Rivers OF Restoration

TROUT UNLIMITED'S
FIRST 50 YEARS OF CONSERVATION

John Ross

Skyhorse Publishing

www.skyhorsepublishing.com

10 9 8 7 6 5 4 3 2 1

Library of Congress Cataloging-in-Publication Data

Ross, John, 1946-
  Rivers of restoration : trout unlimited's first fifty years of
conservation / John Ross.
    p. cm.
  ISBN 978-1-60239-211-3 (hardcover : alk. paper)
  1. Stream restoration—United States. 2. Trout Unlimited. I. Title.

QH76.R665 2008
639.9'77570973—dc22
                        2007049952

Design by Jim Gray and Adam Bozarth
Maps by Timothy Lawrence

Printed in China

Rivers of Restoration is dedicated to Trout Unlimited founder Art Neumann, for his tireless efforts to make TU a national organization; to scores of former and current TU staff who provide the professional expertise and service so vital to achieve our mission; and to hundreds of volunteers like Mike Klimkos, the late Jack Beck, and Inky Moore who established TU's first youth camp and whose vision will perpetuate TU well into the future.

Table of Contents

Preface

A new book on rivers that have been made better is always welcome. No one—the wise old saying goes—is making rivers any more; but the restoration of rivers that have suffered when there were, as John Ross says, "unkind collisions between humankind and the natural environment," is another matter. This is a book about a lot of rivers that have needed help and have gotten it from Trout Unlimited.

When I first fished for trout in the pressured streams of southern New York State in the mid-1950s, we never knew what we'd find after we made the two-hour train trek up from New York City, where there were no trout rivers. Sometimes the river we fished—usually one of those short passages between two reservoirs—would be happily the same except, perhaps, for the shifting of a certain fallen tree that broke the current, which we knew held trout above and below; or the filling of a "hone hole" after a section of road collapsed during a March flood; or a flat stretch now too filled with silt to fish; or a few more brothers of the angle, more each year, killing more and more of the put-and-take stocked trout. It wasn't great trout fishing but we loved it then, and it was all we had. Once I brought a friend to fish a mile or so of river flowing through an empty meadow I'd found and boasted the whole way upcountry that I had once, several years earlier, on a gray morning like this one in early April, taken two of the largest browns I'd ever taken, and surely the largest in the East—one about six pounds, the other three or four. But when we got there we saw that a developer had plunked down at least fifty pre-fabricated houses in that field, a row of them not fifty feet from the river, and there was neither access nor much promise of any fishing. We'd seen nothing worse. But in the years ahead we saw an astonishing growth in the kind and complexity of the threats.

Greed, avarice, ignorance, carelessness—the extent throughout the country of the damage they have done to the clean, cold rivers trout need dwarfs what I saw. Trout Unlimited has been in the forefront of the battle to reverse all that. It cannot do everything, and it has often had to pick its battles, but the group increasingly and in a lot of different ways has done an immense amount, while growing from a few thousand members to a powerful, man-faceted group more than 150,000 strong, and resources ranging from the hard-working members of local chapters to scientists, to fund-raisers, to lawyers capable of arguing against dam-building before the U.S. Supreme Court. The problems they have confronted have often involved America's greatest trout rivers—the Bitterroot, the Blackfoot (so central to Norman Maclean's *A River Runs Through It*), the Deschutes, the Housatonic, the Kennebec, rivers in New York's Catskill mountains, Alaska, the great spring creeks of the Driftless Area of Wisconsin—rivers east and west, north and as far south as the Guadaloupe in Texas, some large, others quite small, freestone, spring creek, whatever will sustain salmonids.

The problems have been a sad litany of the gross mischief some people, governments, and corporations have caused: dam-building, water-release deficiencies that warm a river, over-grazing of cattle that erodes stream banks, toxic discharge from mining, profligate logging, the destruction of fish habitat, and so much more. Surely natural disasters have caused some of the problems, and they have received no less attention.

The effort, over a long period of time, has required a substantial growth in membership to provide the clout needed to address so many of these issues. It has required a constant need to raise substantial sums of money. It has required constant vigilance at both the local and national levels, to identify problems early, and strategies for comprehensive cooperation with businesses and landowners, support of Trout in the Classroom efforts and other educational programs, persistent efforts to broker local economic and environmental cooperation, and practical stream improvements such as the building of fish-habitat structures, often by local chapters.

Rivers of Restoration profiles nearly two dozen rivers and watersheds and frames Trout Unlimited's role in combatting the threats of their health. This important book poignantly shows how the waters have been distressed and how careful stewardship can make a substantial difference. This is a thoughtful, vivid, and ultimately uplifting report from the war zone where the fate of our precious trout rivers is challenged. It is an ongoing battle.

NICK LYONS

Foreword

Nick Lyons is always a tough act to follow. I started reading Nick's books right after college, when I had the good fortune to meet a few people who helped me transform my love of fishing into the passion for fly fishing that has informed many of the waking moments of my adulthood. I grew up fishing different waters than those Nick fished, but the decrepit state of the many of the southern New England rivers I knew as a boy and a young man helped me identify readily with what Nick had to say about eking out serenity and an angler's sense of fulfillment in places that would later benefit from Trout Unlimited's advocacy and stewardship.

John Ross, writing as chronicler of TU's grassroots successes nationwide, is too humble even to mention his own role as a TU volunteer leader. When it comes to Rivers of Restoration, John knows that of which he writes. In addition to sharing with us his skills in documenting TU's success, John has given generously of himself in showing TU's people how they can become engaged in and dedicated to a cause far larger than themselves. John knows as well as anyone that, without that engagement and dedication, there simply would not be much of a tale to tell about the Rivers of Restoration he describes in this book.

Almost a decade ago, as we approached the new millennium, Bruce Babbitt, who served as President Bill Clinton's Secretary of the Interior, described the historical context of our nation's conservation movement. The nineteenth century, he noted, was America's age of discovery, the twentieth century its age of exploitation, and the twenty-first its age of restoration. Although history often eludes such neat delineations, Babbitt's description is pretty accurate. If you think it through, you'll see a similar pattern running throughout each of the subtexts John presents in this book.

I came to TU in 1991, at a time when the organization had experienced some setbacks and itself needed some restoration. My job was to build a national organization of which TU's grassroots activists, who had been toiling pretty much on their own for almost 30 years, could be proud. Raising the needed funds meant making TU more saleable to the fly fishing market and to private foundations, government agency partners, and individual philanthropists. The results of the effort have shaped the tale told in the pages that follow. In addition to its budget and staff growth ($2.5 million to $23 million; 20 people to over 100), TU's volunteer network is stronger than ever.

Trout Unlimited has succeeded because it has never strayed from the philosophy that founding grassroots member Art Neumann articulated 50 years ago, when he observed that, "if we take care of the fish, the fishing will take care of itself." The organization has also succeeded because it has remained faithful to a guiding, if unstated, principle: that its people are every bit as important as the causes it espouses.

Trout Unlimited's people are the force that drives this narrative. Yet at the end of the day, what we pass on to our children and grandchildren is not so much the epic of where we fished and toiled and stood up to be counted, but the rivers themselves. The rivers in this book are some of the quiet places we have sought to protect and restore as "trout waters," that still look and feel the way they did when the world was a bit younger than it is today.

My father first took me fishing for trout in a now-forsaken southern New England stream known to him only as "Grandfather's Falls." There were wild brook trout there, and I caught them without ever knowing that they and their home would soon disappear. Smothered by toxic run-off, its headwaters buried under asphalt and concrete, Grandfather's Falls was lost before it could become a River of Restoration. Thanks, however, to Trout Unlimited's people, many of whose stories this book so ably tells, there are other places we can pass on—with pride and the deep satisfaction of knowing that ours was a job well done—to those who will fish behind us.

CHARLES GAUVIN
President of Trout Unlimited

Introduction

Take a river, any river. It rises in a spring, on the flank of a mountain, where swales coalesce on the prairie. Water emerging gently from the earth is born with such hope, with so much innocence. At first a rivulet, flowing in smooth lamina with its surface etched only by weeping tendrils of grass or merrily skipping from rock to pool to rock the way a child plays hop-scotch, it gathers other waters to it, matures into a stream, and thence becomes a river.

We are all much like rivers, weaned from the waters where we grew up, drawing sustenance from and nourishing, too, the terrain through which we pass. When I stand concentrating on presenting a blue-winged olive to a rainbow gorging on the cloud of naturals where the Henry's Fork runs behind the old A-bar, I have no thought of this. My mind is on the trout and my cast. But when the current presses against my waist as I struggle for a better angle, I cannot help but imagine this water, the journey it must make, and all of the diversions that threaten its run to the sea. We are, each of us, a river.

We are also like the trout that the best rivers hold. We run upstream to where the water is coldest and purest. We seek refuge there, for as Horace Kephart, the great Appalachian chronicler of a century ago, put it: "We get it rough enough in town." Trout are like that as well. Kephart knew the speckled trout—brookies—that lurked beneath hemlock roots high up on Little Fork of Sugar Fork, where he made his home in 1904. He saw them erased, victims of the ravages of logging, from all but the most rugged of the high mountain gorges too steep for early twentieth century man to timber. Like trout in the best of our waters, we swim against the flow in constant search of sanctuary.

Fishing for trout has been good for me. An asthmatic kid, I was taken hold of by Scout Master John Kinsey of Knoxville, Tennessee's Troop 30 and introduced to the environs of the Great Smokies and the waters that flow from their high peaks and balds. We fished the Pigeon, Abrams Creek, Citico, and Tellico from our tent camps, and caught their rainbows and browns with worms and Kounty Kist corn. We canoed the Little Tennessee and the Clinch, cast and waded wet, and slept on beds of honeysuckle in flower. The plethora of colds that plagued me faded. I suppose that I out grew them, but I'll always believe that it was those outings that healed me and sustain me still.

For fifty years, the volunteers of Trout Unlimited have strived to preserve, restore, reconnect, and sustain the nation's trout and salmon waters. In this book, I've attempted to introduce a few places where unkind collisions between humankind and the natural environment are being mitigated. While writing *Rivers*, I was reading George Black's eloquent *The Trout Pool Paradox*. He raised the question of restoration to what end. The clock can only be turned back so far, and it keeps on ticking, always. As anglers, our desires seem almost frivolous. But the work that TU does in reduction of sedimentation and acid mine drainage and the reintroduction of self-sustaining populations of trout is of significant economic and social benefit.

As I toured watersheds where TU has made a difference, I was struck by the great similarity among successes. In every case there was a champion—Don Duff and Pat Coffin and Nevada cutthroat; Steve Moore and the southern Appalachian brook trout; Luki Akelkok, patriarch of the Nushagak; Sharon Lance on the South Platte—whose individual leadership sustained campaigns to achieve the goal. In every instance, success was advanced through partnership with other organizations and through compromise so that every holder of a stake in the watershed received added benefit from the course of action ultimately chosen. Some of the projects, like American Fork, were accomplished in a few years. Most required decades. Conservation is a long haul.

Mike Klimkos of Carlisle, Pennsylvania, lives that commitment. The second son of a miner who stripped coal from the high plateau above the West Fork of the Susquehanna, Mike has devoted a lifetime to repairing, as a professional, the havoc his dad wrought in the Kettle Creek drainage. He also knows that future success can only be ensured if youngsters are hooked early on the union between conservation and angling. That's why he's so adamant about continuing the work of the late Jack Beck and Inky Moore and other members of the Cumberland Valley Chapter, who started the Rivers Conservation and Fly Fishing Youth Camp on the Yellow Breeches Creek at Boiling Springs. Since that camp's founding in 1995, a dozen similar summer camps have been established across the country. These camps, along with hundreds of Trout in the Classroom projects and a new partnership with the four-million-strong Boy Scouts of America, are preparing the next generation of conservation anglers.

Global warming, acid rain, sedimentation, chemical and bacterial pollution, poorly planned development: All are massive challenges to the quality of the nation's cold and pure headwaters. To meet these conservation challenges, there is nothing more important to sustaining the future than the education of our youth.

John Ross
Upperville, Virginia, 2008

American Fork, Utah

 In late October, 1862, with the Union and Confederate armies reeling from the inconclusive battle at Antietam that resulted in more than 23,000 killed and wounded soldiers, the single bloodiest day in American military history, a troop of U.S. Volunteers from California rode into Salt Lake City. Their orders: preserve the Overland Trail and telegraph from Indian attack.

Heading the column was an Irishman, Colonel Patrick Edward Connor, who'd shed his 'O' in 1839 when, as a nineteen-year-old, he enlisted in the regular army in New York. He and his men had no time to lose, as winter comes early to Utah. Instead of building cabins, his soldiers took picks and shovels and carved four-foot-deep dugouts into the ground and covered them with canvas roofs. Each was fitted with an adobe or stone chimney, held twelve men, and was reputed to be quite comfortable when the snow flew.

Connor's soldiers didn't have much to do, as the Indians were not restless. As time permitted, they prospected in the surrounding mountain valleys. Their skills with picks and shovels proved extremely valuable. Connor, himself, is reported to have made the first discovery of silver in Little Cottonwood Canyon, across the Wasatch Mountains from the valley of American Fork.

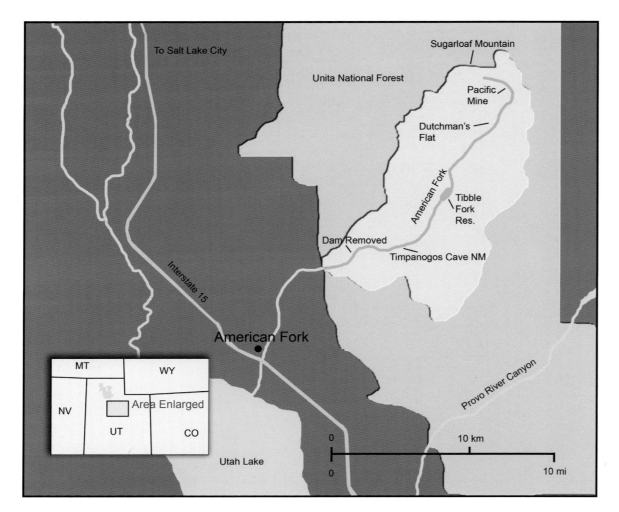

The map labels include: To Salt Lake City, Sugarloaf Mountain, Unita National Forest, Pacific Mine, Dutchman's Flat, American Fork, Tibble Fork Res., Dam Removed, Timpanogos Cave NM, Interstate 15, American Fork, Provo River Canyon, Utah Lake. Inset map: MT, WY, NV, UT, CO, Area Enlarged. Scale: 0 — 10 km; 0 — 10 mi.

What was left were thousands of tons of mine tailings, toxic with astoundingly high concentrations of lead, arsenic, cadmium, and zinc.

The peaks of the ridge—Mount Baldy and Sugar Loaf, which are popular skiing runs at modern-day Snowbird Resort—were veined with lead, silver, and gold. By July 1869, the American Fork Mining District had been established on the southwest side of the mountains, on the headwaters of the river of the same name.

The boom was on. Miners who'd missed out on Sutter's gold and who'd retuned home from the Civil War to find few jobs made their way into the ruggedly steep valley. Some prospected and worked their own claims. Others hired out for as much as $4 per day. Their tools were simple: a shovel, a pick, a $7/8$-inch star drill, and a jack hammer (a short-handled sledge of about three pounds). A miner would hold his drill against the face of the rock with one hand, hit it a good lick with the jack hammer, rotate the drill ninety degrees, then wallop it again.

Day in and day out, through summer and winter, the miners toiled at their work. Snowfall often accumulated to twenty feet, forcing them to burrow through the whiteness from bunk-house, to chow hall, to tunnel, and back again. Some didn't see the sky for months. Avalanches swept other men down slopes. Their bodies were found, thawed, and buried in the spring. Arguments among the well-lubricated were settled by six-shooters. No wonder that Governor Brigham

U.S. Forest Service

Shallow silent ponds, high in the south slopes behind Snowbird Resort, filter drainage from the once booming Pacific Mine. (preceding page)

So productive was Pacific, that by 1916 a mill had been added on the little flat beneath the mine's portal. (left)

American Fork trips over structures in Dutchman's Flat where mounds of poison waste were once piled. (right)

Young urged his flock to eschew the lure of all that glittered and pursue the real riches of farm and family.

Mining along the American Fork bloomed in the 1870s but ultimately succumbed to the deep recession of the last half of that decade. The richest strike was discovered by brothers named Miller, on an 11,000-foot peak named in mock-modesty, "Miller Hill" on the south slope of Hidden Peak Ridge. The Miller Mine faded in 1876, but not before ore worth roughly $540 million (today) had been chiseled from the mountain. By the end of the decade, 780 claims had been staked on nearby slopes.

For the next twenty years, work at the mines slowed but never ceased. New adits were started and old tunnels lengthened. Mining in the district began to revive in the early 1900s with the opening of the Pacific Mine on American Fork at the base of Miller Hill. Peter Miller took over its operation in 1914, believing, apparently, that his predecessor had done little more than turn the top soil. Six months later he'd tunneled in 500 feet and planned to go another 700.

World War I drove lead and precious metal prices skyward. Miners at Pacific struck a large vein of copper and gold ore at just about the same time, ensuring the company's success for years to come. Just one rail car of ore from this vein brought, in today's dollars, $170,000. By 1916, Pacific had added its own mill, and, later that year, it became one of the first operations to receive electric power. Energy came from a small dam far down American Fork, which Trout Unlimited would ultimately have a hand in decommissioning. A filtration plant was added at Pacific in 1918.

Cycling through the boom of the 1920s and a slowdown with the Great Depression, mining provided steady employment through the years for residents of American Fork, Forest City, and Pleasant Grove. Pacific Mine continued to flourish through World War II, but victory killed demand for low-grade ore remaining in Pacific's seams. The mine closed for good in the late 1940s.

What was left, according to Ted Fitzgerald of the U.S. Forest Service, were thousands of tons of mine tailings, toxic with astoundingly high concentrations of lead, arsenic, cadmium, and zinc. Lead poisoning is known to cause brain and kidney damage in children and in adults, problematic pregnancies and nerve disorders. Fitzgerald knew his terrain. For twenty-five years, he'd spearheaded mine reclamation on Western national forests. He came to Uinta National Forest in 1999 cleaning up much of the mess left after the last truckload of ore rumbled down the valley forty years earlier.

As a Forest Service employee, Fitzgerald's problem was this: He could only mitigate toxic tailings and drainage on federal land. But abandoned mines were on private property surrounded by the national forest. For decades, mines had dug their ore and dumped the tailings down the slopes onto public land. The tailings came under the Forest Service's jurisdiction, but the mines on private property did not. Moreover, When Snowbird Resort added Hidden Peak Ridge to its ski slopes, it acquired the old Pacific Mine. Well aware that the cost of mitigating the mine's wastes far exceeded the value of the acreage, the resort was content to let sleeping dogs lie. Yet, since

TU in Action

Created a public-private partnership, developed new tactics and technologies, and raised $280,000 for the cleanup of the Pacific Mine, a model for mitigating pollution at more than 500,000 similar sites in the West.

Spearheaded delicensing and eventual removal of outmoded dam in American Fork Canyon.

US Forest Service

Partners include Tiffany & Company Foundation, Snowbird Ski and Summer Resort, and the Boy Scouts.

outdoor recreation and environmental health are kindred spirits, the presence of Pacific's hazards nettled Snowbird's owners. In 2004, Chris Wood, TU's vice president for conservation, brokered a model public-private partnership that would collect and bury Pacific's tailings in an impervious mound and create a series of ponds to filter drainage seeping from the abandoned mine. A month after Fitzgerald retired from the Forest Service, he was hired by TU to do the job.

A grant from the foundation of Tiffany & Co., which fashions much of its jewelry from gold and silver mined in Utah, paid Fitzgerald's salary for two years. Snowbird contributed heavy equipment and employees to run it. Additional funding came from the Forest Service and other federal sources. In the end, Boy Scouts planted willows around oxidation ponds that filter mine drainage. Fitzgerald's team completed the project in 2006. Citing TU and the partnership as Good Samaritans and the project as a "trail-blazing effort with significant environmental benefit" and a model for mitigating pollution from more than 500,000 abandoned hard-rock mines in the West, the Environmental Protection Agency gave the project its Environmental Achievement Award in 2007. Snowbird won the Golden Eagle Award for Environmental Excellence from the National Ski Areas Association.

How's the Fishing?
With the cleanup of the Pacific Mine, Bonneville cutthroat trout have returned to the upper reaches of American Fork above Tibble Fork Reservoir. Flowing through a tight canyon, the stream is a series of runs, chutes, and pools. Its trout seldom see anglers. Well above the stream runs an incredibly rocky road, so narrow that two SUVs can't pass without folding in their mirrors. Here and there are pullouts where parking is possible and where cars can pass as well. Anglers willing to scramble down the steep slope to the stream will find that they can toss almost any small attractor, dry or brown or grey nymph, and catch fish.

Below Ductchman's Flat, the stream enters a deep and shady gorge. (left top)

CHAPTER 2

Au Sable, Michigan

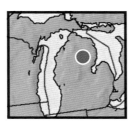 To hear an Easterner tell it, the history of fly fishing in America is hooked to the storied Beaverkill, Neversink, and other waters of the Catskills. But nowhere are the heritage of fly fishing and the conservation of trout and their habitat more deeply intertwined than on Trout Unlimited's home watershed, the Au Sable, and its tributaries.

Trout Unlimited is the result of the coincidental confluence of place, people, and World War II. Well into his forties, too old to fight, and a salesman of fine hosiery when nylon was rationed, George A. Griffith was forced to sit out the conflict on the banks of the Au Sable. Idleness, however, was not his nature, not when it came to the watershed he'd adopted as home.

Griffith made his first trek from his hometown in Lima, Ohio to northern Michigan when he was fifteen, arriving with a gaggle of uncles and cousins. Strapped to the trunk of their touring car were crates of live chickens. A five-gallon can of dried beans was lashed to a running board. For twelve hours, they jostled their way up largely dirt roads and arrived at a cabin near Sage Lake. The boys caught bluegills until they were bored, and eventually extended their range to Klacking Creek where, using a red worm, Griffith caught his first trout, a brookie. That was 1916.

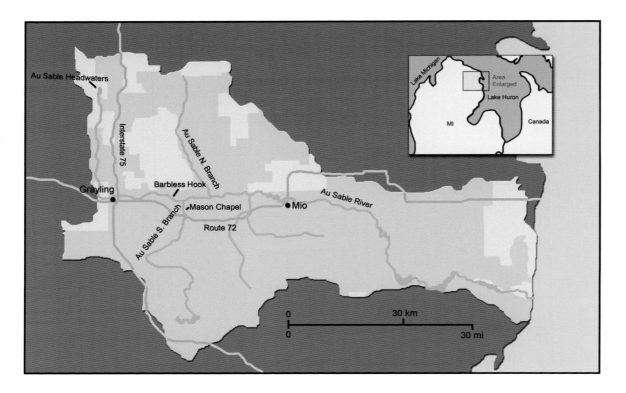

Shortages of gasoline and nylon forced Griffith, a salesman of stockings, to sit out World War II on the banks of the Au Sable.

Thus began a life dedicated to the pursuit of trout. Griffith would casually work fishing or hunting into conversations with anyone he met. Once, while interviewing for a job selling lace trimmings, he asked for Michigan to be included in his territory. When his prospective employer asked why, he responded, "I'm a trout fisherman." "So am I," replied the interviewer, who promptly hired George and invited him on a trip to Traverse City to fish and discuss business.

Ever gregarious, Griffith had more than a salesman's panache. His customers became friends; their friends became his friends; and all joined at the ferrule in their love of Michigan trout fishing and bird hunting. Though he knew of the Au Sable—it had been touted as one of the nation's first-class trout streams as far back as 1896—he didn't get a chance to fish it until July 1934. He and his wife and another couple rendezvoused west of the lumber town of Grayling at Edgewater Lodge by Stephan's Bridge. They hired two guides and their narrow wooden river boats for a four-mile float down to Wakeley Bridge. Foot-long browns and brookies fell to their hoppers all day long. The fish weren't the only thing that got hooked that day.

Two years later, Griffith bought a 24-foot-by-24-foot summer cabin just below Wakeley Bridge. It was a primitive affair, with no running water or electricity, but it was on the Au Sable, and that's all that mattered. With the Japanese bombing of Pearl Harbor on December 7, 1941, came shortages of rayon, nylon, and, most important to Griffith, the gasoline he needed for the trips north to his cabin. Though his company still paid his salary and commissions, stockings were in short supply, and he was only allowed to make two three-week sales trips north each year. The rest of the time he had to sit at home unless he could hook up with somebody with enough gas stamps to fuel a car to Grayling and back. The war was putting a serious crimp in his fishing.

Word was out that George was looking for a year-round place on the river. Earl Madsen, a renowned fly tier and Au Sable guide, told him of a run-down cabin upstream a ways from Wakeley Bridge. George wangled a loan and bought it for $10,000 in 1943. He and his wife took up residence. Still under the travel embargo for the rest of the war and a few years following, he was stuck on the river, working on the cabin, mastering his narrow riverboat bought from John Stephan, and fishing. Poor George. Legendary flyrodder Joe Brooks named the cabin the Barbless Hook.

Griffith learned the lineage of trout on the eight-mile Holy Water stretch of the Au Sable, better than most genealogists know their own family trees. He could tell native fish from wild fish and

Named by Joe Brooks, the Barbless Hook was Griffith's second cabin on the river. He glassed in the front porch, creating the living room, with its splendid view of the Au Sable's Holy Waters. There TU was launched in the summer of 1959.

BIRTHPLACE OF TROUT UNLIMITED

THROUGH THE EFFORTS OF GEORGE A. GRIFFITH AND A GROUP
OF DISTINGUISHED ANGLERS TROUT UNLIMITED WAS FOUNDED
HERE ON THE AU SABLE RIVER ON JULY 18, 1959

TROUT UNLIMITED IS A NATIONAL CONSERVATION ORGANIZATION
DEDICATED TO THE PRESERVATION OF TROUTS AND THEIR ENVIRONMENT
AND THE PERPETUATION OF THE FINE SPORT OF TROUT ANGLING

PRESENTED BY
THE GEORGE M. MASON CHAPTER
TROUT UNLIMITED
JULY 12, 1969

TU was founded to conserve, protect, and restore wild and native trout and their habitats.

both from stockers. It wasn't long after being appointed to the state Conservation Commission in 1949 that he embarked on a campaign to improve the Au Sable and its fish. He'd been a galvanizing force in the organization of the Au Sable River System Property Owners Association.

George Mason, president of American Motors, and owner of fourteen miles of the South Branch of the Au Sable, and Griffith had known each other for more than a decade. Soon after joining the Conservation Commission, Griffith was approached by Mason while both men were waiting to launch boats at Burton's Landing, another stop on the Holy Waters. "As you know, George," Mason said (remembers Griffith in his book *For the Love of Trout*), "I've been national treasurer of Ducks Unlimited since it was organized, but my first love is trout fishing. I have been thinking about a similar organization: Trout Unlimited."

The idea for TU was Mason's, and the first meeting was held at his home on the South Branch in 1950. Among the handful of people present were Don McLouth, founder of McLouth Steel, and Opie Titus, a highly regarded outdoorsman and writer. McLouth felt that one day trout fishing would only be enjoyed by the wealthy. Titus disagreed, stating that "the working man has just as much right to fish for trout as corporation presidents." Also discussed were catch-and-release, practiced then by most Au Sable fly fishers, and fly fishing-only regulations. The concept of stopping stocking programs in favor of improving trout habitat was also talked about. This made excellent sense to Griffith, who was tired of catching puny fish that seldom survived a season and consumed the lion's share of the state's fishery budget.

Mason, ten years Griffith's senior, died in 1954, but not before leaving more than 1,100 acres along the South Branch to the state . . . with the stipulation that it be left in a natural condition. Over the next five years, Griffith and like-minded Au Sable fly fishers labored over just what Trout Unlimited should be and do. McLouth passed away during this period, and the composi-

An excellent tyer, George developed the Griffith's gnat, one of the world's most effective trout patterns. (above)

Commemorated by this monument on TU's 100-acre tract on the Au Sable, Art Neumann authored the philosophy which guides TU today. (right)

tion of TU's founding group ebbed and flowed. In July 1959 the organization seemed ready to hatch. Griffith was still serving as a Conservation Commissioner and was unwilling to move forward without a green light from Governor Soapy Williams.

Griffith got what he wanted and that fall TU was launched under the philosophy penned by founding TU members Art Neumann and E. Sutton:

Trout Unlimited believes that trout fishing isn't just fishing for trout.

It's fishing for sport rather than food where the true enjoyment of the sport lies in the challenge, the love and the battle of wits, not necessarily the full creel.

It's the feeling of satisfaction that comes from limiting your kill instead of killing your limit.

It's communing with nature where the chief reward is a refreshed body and a contented soul, where a license is a permit to use—not abuse, to enjoy—not destroy our trout waters.

It's subscribing to the proposition that what's good for trout is good for trout fisherman and that managing trout for the trout rather than for the fisherman is fundamental to the solution of our trout problems.

It's appreciating our trout, respecting fellow anglers and giving serious thought to tomorrow.

In the years that immediately followed, Neumann, as TU's first vice president, hit the road spreading the TU gospel. By 1962, he was named executive director, a position he held until 1965. His missionary work inspired thirty new chapters and nearly doubled the size of the organization. Says cane rod maker Bob Summers, who often piloted Griffith down the Au Sable, "George got TU up and running, but it was Art who made it a national organization."

Flat-bottomed and hard-chined, Au Sable river boats were designed by lumberjacks whose camp cooks required a stable craft that, laden with provisions, could be easily poled upriver. (right)

How's the Fishing? Open year-round, but subject to special regulations, the best way to sample the Au Sable is in a narrow wooden boat, the way George Griffith did it. I used to be an early-to-bed, early-to-rise kind of guy until TUer Carl Hueter and master cane rod builder John Pickard introduced me to the hex hatch below Mason's Chapel on the South Branch. In the starlight we could see just enough for short casts. There was never any doubt about the strike of those browns! Wading isn't difficult. Or you can float it, arriving by a likely deadfall sweeper just as the day's last light fades. A stout 6-weight is perfect. Buy appropriate flies from one of the local shops. Plan to spend more than one night, 'cause the browns don't always cooperate. And if you're a first-timer, hiring a guide is well worth the hole it puts in your wallet.

Russ Schnitzer

Griffith often fished with rod-maker Bob Summers who insists: "George got TU up and running, but it was Art Neumann who made it a national organization."

C H A P T E R   3

Bitterroot River, Montana

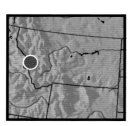

Drought and the Great Depression rolled hand in hand across Montana in the 1930s. And so on the headwaters of the West Fork of the Bitterroot River, named for the state flower of red and blue with roots essential to the diets of native Salish and Kootenai Indians, Painted Rocks Dam was constructed to provide jobs and water for irrigation, life-blood of the region's agrarian economy. Of earthen fill, 800 feet long and 143 feet high, the dam impounds a lake covering 655 acres, or just over a square mile.

Painted Rocks was unusual among western water projects. Though the 100-mile-long Bitterroot Valley was the first in Montana to draw permanent white settlers, ranching was not well developed in the valley when the dam was completed in 1939. There was no great demand for its water. Flows from Painted Rock were sold on short-term twelve-year contracts, sort of like oil on the spot market, as a hedge against the higher prices that the water would command once the depression was over and the valley's economic engine began firing on all cylinders.

Agriculture picked up steam in the valley after World War II. Demands on the Bitterroot, once teeming with native Westslope cutthroat and bull trout, increased apace. Today, Ravalli and southern Missoula counties, through which the river flows, are among the state's most rapidly growing population centers. Real estate and construction rank highly on the list of the counties' economic drivers. So too does tourism. Anglers arrive by the droves. The 10,000-foot Bitterroot and Sapphire mountains that frame the valley attracted hikers and hunters of elk and mule deer. Recreation businesses—guides, motels, restaurants, gas and convenience stores—continue to flourish. Fueling that motor is the demand for water, for which, unlike coal or oil, there exists no alternative, maintains Laura Ziemer, director of TU's Montana Water Project.

Stored behind Painted Rocks aging earth-fill dam was a reservoir of cold, wet cash. By the mid-1950s, farmers were diverting the river to irrigate their fields. Sewage, some of it treated, was dumped into the river. In 1958, the Montana Department of Fish, Wildlife and Parks purchased

If permanent water rights were not secured, pressures
from development, agriculture, and global warming
would put them out of reach . . . forever.

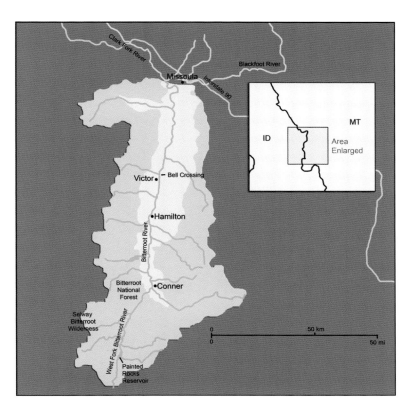

perpetual rights to 5,000 acre feet of lake water to maintain in stream flows. That wasn't enough. By the 1970s the river was in trouble. At times in the early 1980s, sections of the river became completely dry. The department bought additional water to protect the fish, but in 1985 and other drought years, the augmented flows barely dampened Bell Crossing, forty-eight miles downstream from the dam.

Hamilton physician-scientist, Marshall Bloom, was exercised to say the least. He'd led the campaign to restore fluvial grayling in the Big Hole and would later chair the state's Whirling Disease Task Force. In the mid-1980s he'd moved from presidency of the Bitterroot Chapter of Trout Unlimited to chair of the state council. He and former Fish and Wildlife Director Pat Graham were acutely aware that, though a water manager had been hired to ensure that agricultural and recreational interests each received their entitled flows, simply not enough water was being released to go around. He knew well that in 1992 a new round of twelve-year water leases would be signed. He and members of the chapter and council pushed and prodded, nettled and cajoled, and secured an additional 10,000 acre feet for the river through 2004. At the same time, the chapter was deeply involved in stream-bank stabilization and other habitat restoration projects.

Negotiations for the 2004 round of short-term water leases began in the late 1990s. That's when Laura Ziemer, director of TU's Montana Water Project, appeared on the scene. She's a new breed of lawyer-conservationist, smart and passionate about sustaining natural resources and savvy in navigating the political shoals and chutes that separate federal and state agencies charged with protecting the environment.

There's more here than a green legal beagle. Laura makes it sound so simple when she tells you this. Lithe and limber, it's not hard to believe that she was a professional climbing ranger at North Cascades National Park who specialized in search and rescue. In 1995, she and her physician boyfriend were selected as members of an American expedition to retrace George Mallory's climb up the north ridge of Mt. Everest in an attempt to determine whether the man who retorted "Because it's there" when asked why he wanted to climb the mountain ever made it to the top.

Digging her pick in here, finding a toe-hold there, avoiding the rotten ice, skirting crevasses, and making progress is probably a hyperbolic description of Laura's campaign to secure perpetual flows for the Bitterroot. But that's just want she did after opening TU's Montana Water Project in 1998. Shortly thereafter, Laura met Marshall, and he told her to pay attention to Painted Rocks water. If permanent rights to adequate flows are not secured by 2004, he said, pressures from development, agriculture, and global warming would put them out of reach . . . forever.

Conflicting views prevailed about the best use for Painted Rocks water. Fish, Wildlife and Parks championed the fishery. The Department of Natural Resources said fish are nice but jobs and paychecks are more important. At TU's behest, the Columbia Basin Water Transactions Program—a player because one of the conditions for construction of Bonneville Dam is mitigation of negative impacts on native species—funded a study that documented that recreational angling added nearly $600,000 annually to the economic base in the Bitterroot Valley. To maintain the fishery and its income and to reestablish endangered bull trout, Fish and Wildlife argued that ample water must reach Bell Crossing during persistent dry spells in late summer.

Shuttling between offices with the aplomb of Henry Kissinger, Laura and her colleague Stan

TU in Action

10,000 acre feet of Painted Rocks water purchased.

100 CFS flows guaranteed at Bell Crossing to preserve habitat.

$1.5 million raised from TU and other sources.

Brokered new partnership among Painted Rocks Water Users Association; Montana's Fish, Wildlife and Parks Commission and Natural Resource Conservation Service; and Trout Unlimited.

Set precedent for establishing the economic value of recreation in computing the worth of water.

Bradshaw—with able assists from Montana TU Executive Director Bruce Farling and continuing guidance from Marshall—were able to bridge the chasm between the agencies. Their concurrence resulted in a commitment of $1.5 million to secure 10,000 acre feet of Painted Rocks water in perpetuity, enough to ensure 100 cfs (cubic feet per second) flows during periods of drought or high temperature at Bell Crossing. The agreement was signed in 2004, just days before the temporary agreement of 1992 would have expired.

On a scorching July afternoon not long ago, I stood at Bell Crossing. Drought held much of Montana, Oregon, and Idaho in its cindering grip. Wild fires browned the sky with smoke. Yet on the gravel bar upstream of the bridge, families picnicked and swam in the cold river. A little farther on, where the road crosses one of the Bitterroot valley's sloughs, a squadron of cutts glided in and out of tendrils of moss, waving in the current. Downstream a bit, Andy Carlson a river guide and former Bitterroot chapter president, was concluding a float trip for clients, happy with the cutts they'd just caught and released. For the time being, the Bitterroot is back.

How's the Fishing?

If you have one shot to fish the Bitterroot, make it during the skwala hatch. Beginning in March, the emergence of these great big stoneflies continues into May. The river is apt to be swollen with snowmelt, but no matter. Drift the river, cast Chernobyl foam patterns against every likely looking rock on the bank. Cutts are so eager to seize your fly, it's hard to miss. Every ten miles or so, is a public access site. My favorite run is from Poker Jo down to Bell Crossing. Walk the river up or down to find water that appeals, but stay below the ordinary high-water level. Montanans, like everyone else, want respect for their private property rights.

Huge stoneflies (Skwala parallela) open the Bitterroot's best fishing in March, when spring first scents the valley air.

CHAPTER 4

Blackfoot River, Montana

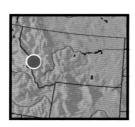 "On the Big Blackfoot River above the mouth of Belmont Creek, the banks are fringed by large Ponderosa pines. In the slanting sun of late afternoon, the shadows of great branches reached from across the river, and the trees took the river in their arms. The shadows continued up the bank, until they included us." —Norman Maclean in *A River Runs Through It and Other Stories*

Published in 1976, Maclean's was a memory of the river in 1910, when it teemed with heavy bull trout and Westslope cutthroats, when roads were dirt, mine towns were booming, forests were inexhaustible, and few cattle knew fences. Yet within a decade after Maclean's novella won the Pulitzer Prize, shadows had all but captured the Big Blackfoot. The 1975 failure of the tailings dam at Mike Horse gold mine sluiced millions of gallons of aggressively toxic lead-, copper-, and zinc-rich sediments into the headwaters of the Blackfoot. The poisonous plume deadened the river for ten miles downstream.

Cattle, grazing over the rolling kames and kettles of the river's middle valley, trampled the banks of hundreds of miles of tributaries, nursery waters for bull and cutthroat trout named *Oncorhynchus clarki lewisi* by Meriwether Lewis when he went up the river in 1806. Gone were the alders

Brian Grossenbacher

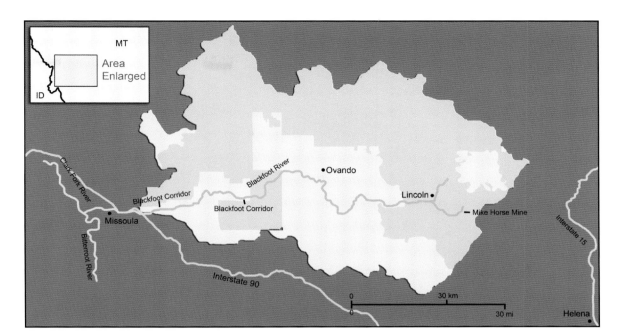

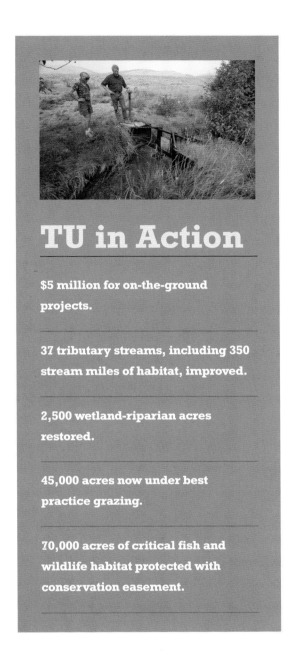

TU in Action

$5 million for on-the-ground projects.

37 tributary streams, including 350 stream miles of habitat, improved.

2,500 wetland-riparian acres restored.

45,000 acres now under best practice grazing.

70,000 acres of critical fish and wildlife habitat protected with conservation easement.

Blowout of the dam at Mike Horse mine in 1975 sluiced thousands of tons of toxic sediments into Norman Maclean's favorite river. In the headwaters and the minds of valley residents, the scars remain. (left)

The twenty-eight-mile Blackfoot River Recreation Corridor provides easy access for anglers who wade. (right)

and willows that cooled the water with shade. Buried under stifling mud were the cobbles where the cutts once spawned and the rocks under which mayfly, caddis, and stonefly larvae grew into food for fingerlings.

Logging had stripped timber from steep ridges and thunderstorms washed what little soil there was into the headwater tributaries, choking them to infertility. Annual droughts became more frequent, limiting flows and increasing competition for what water there was. The Big Blackfoot, all 132 miles of it from the Continental Divide to its confluence with the Clark Fork River south of Missoula, was hearing the bells toll.

Yet Big Blackfoot had one thing going for it: a culture of cooperation partnership among families who care for the river and the land. About the time Maclean's novella was at the publishers, Blackfoot valley rancher Land Lindbergh, the third of Anne and Charles's six children, together with friends Jim Stone and Bill and Betty Potter banded together in 1976 to preserve twenty-six miles of the river's lower canyon. They created, by mutual agreement of landowners, a strip of fifty feet on both banks to ensure public access. Neither Lindbergh, Stone, nor either of the Potters was what you might call an angler, let alone devout. Their prescience, simply put, saved the mileage Maclean, his brother Paul, and minister father so loved to fish. Lindbergh, Stone, and the Potters gave birth to the Blackfoot Recreation Corridor.

A decade went by. Then the Sunshine Mining Co., evidently hoping that the memory of Mike Horse had faded, proposed an open-pit operation to strip gold not 200 yards from the Blackfoot and then leach the precious metal from the ore with cyanide. This, they claimed, was not environmentally hazardous. That got Darryl and Sherry Parker's attention. Their ranch outside of Lincoln was less than half a mile from the proposed mine.

Agitated, Darryl vented his spleen to friend Becky Garland, co-owner of Garland's Town & Country Store in Lincoln. No stranger to the conservation wars (her dad Cecil worked to establish the Scapegoat Wilderness north of the town), Becky was equally incensed at the very idea of a gold mine, though she knew it meant jobs and money in a town where both were scarce.

Darryl also enlisted outfitter Paul Roos and, together with Becky and more than forty neighbors, formed the Big Blackfoot Chapter of Trout Unlimited. Becky was the workhorse. She combed public records and discovered that Sunshine's Kellogg, Idaho, silver mine had been cited for eighty-five water-quality violations. She enlisted ranchers, state agencies, conservation groups, and local businesses in a campaign to shut out Sunshine. Its proposal faded and died.

But the blood it boiled rallied Blackfoot TUers to do something about the fishery as well. Big Blackfoot was then, in the 1980s, pretty modest when compared to most other rivers in Montana's repertoire. The TU chapter had its work cut out for them. Because the state was scant on funds, the chapter raised $16,000 to fund Fish, Wildlife and Parks's studies of the Blackfoot, its problems and potential. The river's recovery had begun.

Always coiled and eager to strike, mining reared its head again four years later when Phelps-Dodge served up an even grander scheme to leach $175 million in gold from claims spanning forty-four miles around Lincoln. It would have been one of the largest cyanide heap-leach gold mines in the country. The company said it planned to operate for about a dozen years. Becky, Paul, and the Blackfoot TU board thought, "Then what?" They'd been through boom and bust cycles in the past. Ghost towns don't become that way without a reason.

Though the Blackfoot watershed covers 1.5 million acres, folks who live along it are a pretty close knit group and they share a common belief. Says third-generation farmer Randy Mannix, "My grandfather, he didn't think of himself as a land owner. He saw himself as a steward of the land." That philosophy, coupled with the ever-pragmatic notion that one can accomplish more through cooperation than individual interest has led conservation forces, including the TU chapter, to collaborate in a very successful, multi-faceted habitat, agricultural practice, economic development, and education collaborative called the Blackfoot Challenge.

In pursuit of its mission to coordinate efforts to enhance, conserve, and protect the natural resources and rural lifestyles of the Blackfoot River Valley for present and future generations, the Challenge has accomplished a great deal, increasing land in conservation easements, reducing conflicts between wildlife and humans, establishing a community-based long-term plan for the regions, and engaging schools and more than sixty stakeholders in the effort.

Maclean, were he reincarnated, wouldn't find the bruising bull trout he used to catch, or swarms of eager Westslope cutthroats. And he'd be put off by the flotillas of rafters and driftboats that ply the river every summer weekend. Yet in the evenings, when lavender chases the alpen glow up the mountains and the days' last best hatches emerge, you'll hear in the ponderosa pines above Belmont Creek the soft *swish swish* of his cane rod.

> Big Blackfoot was then, in the 1980s, pretty modest when compared to most other rivers in Montana's repertoire. The TU chapter had their work cut out for them.

How's the Fishing?

While many anglers float the river for convenience, the best fishing generally comes to those willing to walk and wade. Numerous public access points are located along the river. Among the best are those within the Blackfoot Recreation Corridor. Begin at Johnsrud and work your way upstream until you find water to your liking. Spring run-off leaves the system by mid-June. Follow the last of the melt down from the Continental Divide. Salmon flies and golden stones appear as the melt leaves the valley. Green drakes start about the same time. They're followed by pale morning duns. Caddis and midges always seem to be present, and you'll find tricos in August and baetis in September. Check for new fishing regulations when you buy your license.

Thanks to landowners like Randy Mannix and his son (left) and staff of Montana Fish, Wildlife and Parks, native westslope cutthroats are repopulating the Blackfoot.

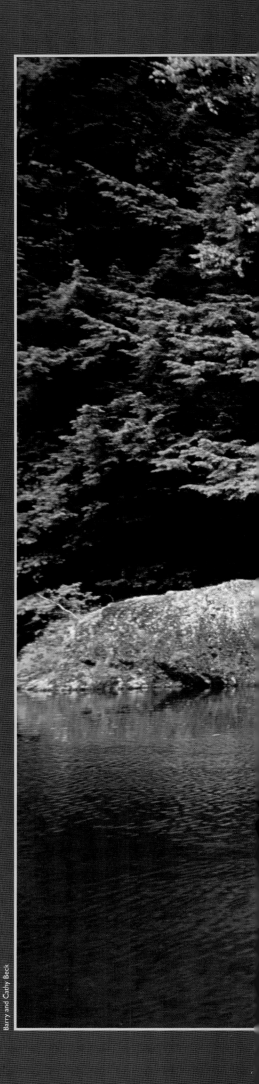

Barry and Cathy Beck

CHAPTER 5

Catskill Rivers
(Beaverkill, Willowemoc, Delaware), New York

No height of land has woven itself so deeply into the fabric of American fly fishing as the Catskill Mountains. An elevated plateau rather than a range of mountains, the Catskills span more terrain than Connecticut. Its tranquil ridges, forested once more now that the tanneries, acid distilleries, and sawmills are gone, are so riven with freestone streams that every valley holds a trove of trout, previously native brookies of five pounds or more, but today largely browns and rainbows. The names—Esopus Creek, Neverskink, Beaverkill, Willowemoc, the Delaware—are as well known to anglers as their own.

Little more than 100 miles northwest of New York City, the waters of the Catskills have attracted legions of fishing writers. Among the first was Washington Irving. Along with "Rip Van Winkle" and "The Legend of Sleepy Hollow," *The Sketch-Book of Geoffrey Crayon, Gent.* contains "The Angler." Irving penned it following his return from Wales in 1818, where he'd attempted to trace the footprints of Izaak Walton.

Prior to 1994, the response to the flooding of Catskill streams had been to straighten their channels.

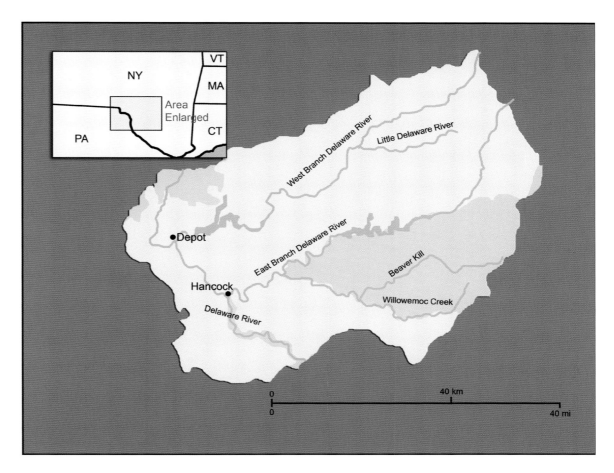

Catskill Fly Fishing Center and Museum

Legions of Catskill anglers trooped into the front room of Harry and Elsie Darbee's house to buy flies. Their ties and those of their friends, Walt and Winnie Dette, were direct descendants of patterns that Theodore Gordon evolved from English examples. (above)

Like all good fishing writers, Irving presented himself modestly: "For my part, I was always a bungler at all kinds of sport that required either patience or adroitness, and had not angled above half an hour before I had completely 'satisfied the sentiment,' and convinced myself of the truth of Izaak Walton's opinion, that angling is something like poetry—a man must be born to it. I hooked myself instead of the fish, tangled my line in every tree, lost my bait, broke my rod, until I gave up the attempt in despair, and passed the day under the trees reading old Izaak . . ."

You know the wet-booted, cane-wielding literati who plied the Catskill streams: Ray Bergman, Sparse Grey Hackle, John Burroughs, Ernest Schwiebert, Ed Van Put, and a brigade of others. Their prose drew a century of fishers to this still bucolic mecca. They came to cast flies tied by the disciples of Theodore Gordon, who translated Frederic Halford's English dry flies and tactics into a language that resonates still with American trout. His lessons and patterns were refined by Roy Steenrod (sire of the Hendrickson) and Walt and Winnie Dette and their good friends Harry and Elsie Darbee. Their flies hooked three generations of Catskill pilgrims and decorated unfathomable numbers of streamside boughs.

They came to fish rods by H. L. Leonard and Ed and Jim Payne and to learn casting from the likes of Lee and Joan Wulff, icons whose academy upstream from Lew Beach schooled an army of anglers who absolutely will never, not ever, break their wrists when casting a fly. They hung their waders on pegs on the shady porches of clubs belonging to the Brooklyn Fly Fishers and Lady Flyfishers Club and great guest houses beginning with Milo Barber's Inn, which opened for anglers on the upper Esopus in 1830, Art Flick's Westkill Tavern, and Trout Valley Farm. They ate prodigiously at beaneries such as the Roscoe Diner, where no one thinks of counting calories any more than they would attempt to number the scales of a trout.

In the 1920s, as Catskill fly fishing was in its golden age, New York City's thirst for riparian recreation led to changes being made to the region's waters. In 1915, the Esopus was dammed by the Ashokan Reservoir. The Schoharie's turn came in 1926 when its water was diverted into the

Esopus. Famed Neversink beats fished by Gordon and Hewitt were flooded with the closure of its dam in 1950.

Then came the Delaware's turn. Rising in the western Catskills, the Delaware serves first as the border between Pennsylvania and (first) New York and (then) New Jersey. Little sibling to the Hudson and Connecticut, the Delaware was coveted by cities such as Trenton, which boasted "Trenton Makes, the World Takes," and Philadelphia. The three states began squabbling over the river in 1925, with headwaters towns incensed that the cities' demands would leave them with no water for residents, their own industrial aspirations, or even the ability to flush their own sewage.

Fish were not an issue. Bass were first stocked in 1870, and Atlantic salmon were introduced in 1871. A few years later, salmon from the Pacific were added. In 1880, a train wreck near Callicoon Creek prompted the brakeman, Dan Cahill, to dump milk cans full of rainbow trout into the river. They thrived, but only when the main river was cool enough; otherwise they headed up the tributaries. Periodic floods drove trout stocked in the tributaries into the main stem as well. Until the 1950s, fishing in the upper reaches of the Delaware was a lot like sitting down to a potluck supper.

All that was about to change. In 1931, the United States Supreme Court ruled that the states through which the Delaware flowed must agree on the use of its waters. This was in the middle of the Depression and the economy was on the ropes. Industrial and political interests were inseparable and drove policies that governed the use of the river. Two cataclysmic hurricanes and the resulting devastation in 1955 sealed the river's fate. Pepacton Dam was completed on the East Branch of the Delaware in 1961, and flows on the West Branch became subject to downstream needs with the closing of Cannonsville Reservoir in 1967.

As a result, eleven miles of the East Branch below Pepacton, seventeen miles of the West Branch down from Cannonsville, and the twenty-seven-mile run from their junction at Hancock to Callicoon were transformed into some of the best trout water in the country. The cold flows provide tremendous habitat and hatches and foster plentiful populations of large browns in the branches

TU in Action

TU's first Home Rivers Initiative created the model for integrating economic and environmental data to protect a watershed.

Since 1994, similar initiatives would be instituted on the Upper Boise River, Potomac headwaters, Bear River, American Fork, South Fork Snake River, Jefferson River, Kettle Creek, West Fork Kickapoo River, and the Upper Connecticut River.

TU also played a lead role the development of the new water management plan for the Delaware.

In 1916, Catskill angler Roy Steenrod noticed
fish gorging on a fly he'd never seen before.
He tied a few imitations and named them for
his friend, A. E. Hendrickson.

The Catskills are once more the source of innovation, but this time it's conservation, not tackle or technique.

and rainbows in the main river. The rainbows are especially vivacious, rivaling young steelhead with their somersaulting leaps and lightning runs.

Great fishing draws anglers, and anglers spend money. They've become a steady source of income for the Catskills, plagued like so many mountain regions with the economic depression that follows the inevitable collapse of unfettered timbering and other industries that extract wealth from natural resources. Declining populations of rainbows and browns in the Beaverkill and Willowemoc led to the creation of Trout Unlimited's first Home Rivers Initiative in 1994. Fourteen more have followed across the country.

Prior to 1994, the response to the flooding of Catskill streams had been to straighten their channels. Today, thanks to the willingness of local government, state and federal agencies, and funders to consider advice from TU staffers, especially Nat Gillispie, whose roots in the region are as thick as the mountains' lush forests, streams are being returned to their natural courses and development in flood plains is being curtailed. In 1996, TU piloted its first assessment of the economic impact from recreational angling. The study showed that anglers added $8 million annually to local economies. In 2007, TU was a key sponsor of a new Delaware water management strategy to bring increased flows in spring and summer, thus benefiting shad and trout populations and the bringing of attendant financial benefits from the anglers who fish for them.

Little more than a century after American fly fishing took root in the Catskills, the mountain streams are once more the source of innovation, this time the integration of good fisheries science with sound economic and social principles that will ensure the long-term viability of the river as a source of clean water and great angling.

Nymphing works well in the runs of the West Branch of the Delaware. (left)

How's the Fishing? The classic fishing on the Beaverkill and Willowemoc begins in mid-April with the Hendrickson hatch. Bring your 5-weight, your Gore-Tex, fleece, waders, a box of nymphs, and Kleenex. Optically challenged anglers like me appreciate the first two weeks of June when big No. 8 green and brown drakes hatch on the West Branch of the Delaware. For those who are fans of the most delicate tippets and tiniest flies, No. 24 tricos and pseudocleons begin coming off in late June and continue into November. Alas, walk-in access is increasingly limited throughout the Catskills.

CHAPTER 6

Clyde River, Vermont

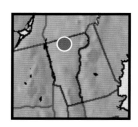

Swiss-born Harvard professor Louis Agassiz, the "first" to understand that glaciers and not the biblical flood sculpted North America, was also the first to identify that a large, dark-backed, silver-sided salmon taken in Maine's Lake Sebago in 1854 was an Atlantic salmon that had adapted to a strictly freshwater environment. Though a staunch opponent of Darwinism to his death, Agassiz found no contradiction between his own philosophy that held that each species was the "thought of God" and his new scientific understanding that *Salmo salar sebago* evolved from its anadromous forbear.

A century would pass before scientists understood how Atlantic salmon came to be landlocked in four lakes in Maine and a handful in Quebec. The weight of thousands of meters of glacial ice had pressed down the surface of the earth. As the glaciers retreated, the sea flowed in, bringing Atlantic salmon along for the ride. Comparable to an ice cube floating in a glass of water, the earth's crust floats on a hot mantel of nearly molten rock. When the weight of the glacial ice was removed, the land slowly rose and trapped Atlantic salmon in lakes they could not have entered by rivers.

Though roughly two-thirds the size of their marine progenitors, landlocked salmon exhibit all the acrobatics and slashing runs that earned Atlantics the sobriquet "fish of kings." Only here in America, one didn't have to be royalty or even wealthy to fish for landlocked salmon. That holds true from the time they were named by Agassiz until today. The last decades of the 1800s and the early 1900s saw a frenetic race to plant trout and salmon in any water that appeared cold enough and clean enough to hold them. Lake Memphremagog, shared by Quebec and Vermont, received its first stocking of landlocks in 1905.

That they thrived is an understatement. No town became more renowned for its landlocked runs than Newport, Vermont, where the Clyde River enters Lake Memphremagog. A writer for *Vermont Life* put it this way in 1950: "Detroit may boast of its autos, Pittsburgh of its steel mills, and Boston of its beans, but up Newport way it's salmon that bust vest buttons and make local chests puff out." In spring, landlocks charge up the Clyde, stuffing themselves on smelt spawning in the river. They return again in the fall to spawn themselves. In the first decades of the century, anglers stood shoulder to shoulder on the town's railroad bridge to fish the spring surge. Each coughed up a nickel for minnows and cast baited hooks and heavy lead weights into rushing water colored like root beer. Hotels and restaurants were filled with fishermen who came, not just from Boston or New York, but from overseas as well.

Newport's heyday as a destination for anglers reached full bloom in the 1920s and '30s, waned during World War II, and died in 1957 when Citizens Utility completed its fourth and final dam, No. 11, on the Clyde. With hubris that would be almost unimaginable today and despite spirited opposition, the company began construction without

"Detroit may boast of its autos, Pittsburgh of its steel mills, and Boston of its beans, but up Newport way it's salmon that bust vest buttons and make local chests puff out."

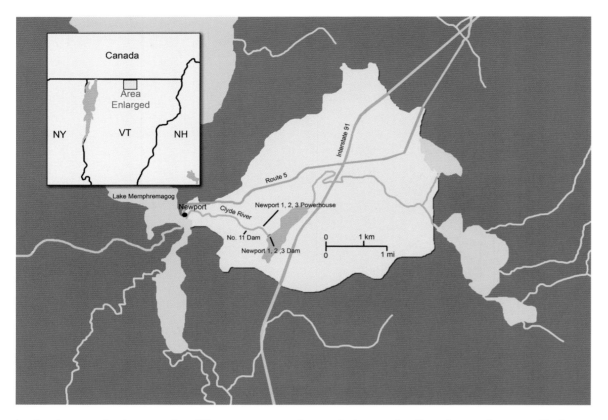

bothering to obtain permits. The state granted permission only after the work was well along. The dam itself was not large at nineteen feet high and ninety feet long. It added less than 2,000 kilowatts of capacity, a pittance even then. The dam essentially dried up 2,100 feet of river channel where salmon had spawned.

The status quo remained until late April 1994, when rain fell for several days on the last of the winter's snow, forcing the Clyde into flood. A seep appeared at the left abutment where the concrete dam joined the clay-rich bank. The seep soon grew into a rivulet, and by the morning of May 1 that rivulet had become a rampaging cataract that rapidly ate away the hillside. Spawning gravels long overgrown with weed and dry troughs and hollows in the original riverbed were suddenly filled with water. Anglers were elated. Nature had achieved what sound reason had not, and the Clyde began to flow freely again. Salmon began to return.

Timing is everything. Five years before No. 11 failed, Citizens Utility had applied to the Federal Energy Regulatory Commission (FERC) to relicense the structure for fifty more years. But the game had changed. In 1986, the FERC had been ordered to evaluate environmental impacts, not just the project's economic benefits. And, just two days before the dam's blow-out, Vermont had officially joined the U.S. Fish and Wildlife Service and Trout Unlimited in urging that relicensing not be granted and that the dam be removed because the sportfishery for landlocks and walleye was worth more to Newport's sagging economy than electricity generated by the dam. Nine months later, the FERC expressed a similar opinion.

The agency's recommendation was precedent-setting. In agreeing with the State of Vermont and Trout Unlimited, the FERC opened the door for challenges to other dams on other rivers as well. The FERC's change of heart, as well as Vermont's official support, did not just happen.

According to John Dillon's 1995 article in *Trout Magazine*, "Heroes of the Clyde," a dedicated core of activists from TU's Northeast Kingdom chapter—Kevin and Karen Coffee, school teacher Gary Ward, storekeeper Dave Smith, and Richard Nelson, dairy farmer and chapter president— waged an unyielding campaign. Their river clean-ups, flow monitoring, and consensus building among sportsmen's clubs, city and county governments, state and federal agencies, and elected officials at state and national levels provided the foundation for FERC's landmark decision.

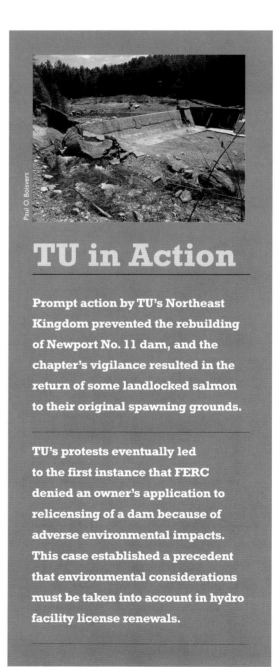

TU in Action

Prompt action by TU's Northeast Kingdom prevented the rebuilding of Newport No. 11 dam, and the chapter's vigilance resulted in the return of some landlocked salmon to their original spawning grounds.

TU's protests eventually led to the first instance that FERC denied an owner's application to relicensing of a dam because of adverse environmental impacts. This case established a precedent that environmental considerations must be taken into account in hydro facility license renewals.

FERC's recommendation was precedent setting. In agreeing with the State of Vermont and Trout Unlimited, the agency opened the door for challenges to other dams on other rivers.

Citizens Utility did not take this lying down. Despite the state's call for removing the dam after it burst, the company immediately began to rebuild it. Citizens said it was merely shoring up the eroded bank. Nelson photographed heavy equipment working in the river channel, was which illegal since the company had again not bothered to get the necessary permits. Testimony from Nelson and others eventually earned a stop-work order from the EPA and construction was halted.

Unwilling to relinquish its grasp on 2,000 kilowatts of generating potential in the lucrative peak-power market, Citizens next tried an end run around state regulators. The company sought permission to build a penstock (a huge enclosed aqueduct) to the No. 11 powerhouse in Newport from its next dam upstream at the outflow of Clyde Pond. Seeking to avoid public hearings and the opposition that was sure to come, the company tried to broker a secret agreement with the state. Vermont's then–secretary of natural resources, Barbara Ripley was as adamant in her letter denying that any agreement had been reached as she was in her insistence that "everyone" be involved. The proposed penstock would have once again dewatered the Clyde's salmon spawning habitat. Public outcry silenced the scheme.

The battle continued. Citizens Utility was acquired by Great Bay Hydro, which planned to wet the Clyde riverbed with a minimum flows 30 cfs, and to trap and truck migrating salmon around their favored spawning beds. In 2004, the Vermont Natural Resources Council filed suit in Vermont's Supreme Court, charging that the plan was insufficient. But in 2006 the court sided with the utility. It ruled that there was scant if any evidence that trout or salmon had spawned in the section of river dewatered by the dam, that artificial means of transporting fish provided a better remedy than attempting to reestablish spawning in the area of the old No. 11 dam, and that the flow of 30 cfs would provide a fishery for spawning landlocks. With their opinion, Vermont's venerable solons stripped the buttons from the vests of anglers seeking Newport's legendary landlocks.

Paul O. Boisvert

How's the Fishing?

Were I headed for the Clyde, I'd shoot for April, when landlocks enter the river to feed on smelt, or October when spawners attempt to run upstream. The pool and bend just below the powerhouse for 1, 2, and 3 dams is the best water, but the river is fishable all the way down to the lake. Traditional streamer patterns, including bushy bead-head woolly buggers tied with a bit of sparkle fished across and down on a 6-weight system, will do the trick. No need for sinking lines in the run below the powerhouse. The water ain't that deep 'til you get to town.

CHAPTER 7

Cutthroats of the Basin, Nevada

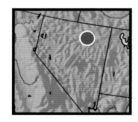Every year or so, I fly into Salt Lake City. From the air, the breathtaking contrast between the broad flat extent of the lake's basin and the soaring peaks of the Wasatch Mountains always stuns me. And when I drive into the city from the airport, or south toward the mouth of the Provo for a date with its browns, my eye is always drawn to a series of terraces high up on the tawny flanks of the foothills. Horizontal geology would explain the fact that the benches occur at the same elevations all along the western slopes of the mountains, but the geology here is much more troubled. To me the terraces look like ancient beaches, evidence of a historic lake that must have been extremely deep.

It wasn't until I hooked up with Don Duff on the west side of the Bonneville Salt Flats last July that my suspicions were confirmed. As we drove out from West Wendover, Nevada, heading south toward the Goshutes Indian Reservation to view his cutthroat restoration project, Duff, who retired from the U.S. Forest Service as a senior aquatic ecologist and has chaired Utah's TU Council, told me about the lake that once occupied the basin. At that time, the northeastern and midwestern United States were buried under thousands of feet of glacial ice.

Called Lake Bonneville, it was 325 miles long, 135 miles wide, and more than 1,000 feet deep. With a surface area of roughly 20,000 square miles, it was only a little smaller than Lake Huron is today. The lake came into being about 32,000 years ago. Then, about 14,000 years before the present, the global warming that terminated the last glacial advance in the Midwest also caused Bonneville's waters to rise, flood, eat through Red Rock Pass, and burst into the valley of the Snake River releasing a catastrophic flood that lasted more than a year and lowered the level of the lake by 325 feet. It's been losing water ever since.

Our route to the Goshutes Reservation took us south across the high desert steppe of short grasses spotted with tufts of greasewood and sage. We drove for ninety miles, sometimes crossing ancient terraces of the lake and at other times dropping down into a valley floor so dry that spit, could I have mustered it up, would probably have evaporated before it hit the ground. It was difficult imagining the herds of prehistoric camels, antelope, mammoths, and bison that used to live here, all of them prey to fleet-footed cheetahs and long-legged, short-faced bears that lived in the open forests of pine and juniper and the boreal meadows of leafy grasses and shrubs and bright wildflowers. Harder still was picturing Bonneville cutthroats the size of Pacific salmon. Today, those Bonneville cutts seldom grow much bigger than ten to twelve inches.

The desiccation of Lake Bonneville, or more correctly its largest remnant, Great Salt Lake, reached its lowest point in the 1963. A decade later, Don was searching for native cutthroats in the Deep Creek Mountains along the border of Utah and Nevada. Leaders on the Goshute Indian Reservation told him, one day, of the fish that once swam in their

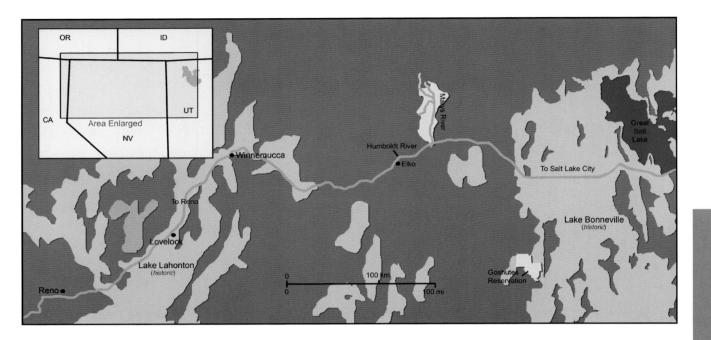

streams. They called them "*ainka painkwi*," literally "red fish." They told him of the importance of the fish. To catch them, elders would take boys up into the mountains to camp. At night the elders would tell the stories of the Goshutes and of what it meant to be a man. The leaders lamented that now, without their red fish, the fishing trips had stopped and with it the traditional way of introducing young men into the culture of the tribe. A year passed and then Duff, who had thought that Bonneville cutthroats were extinct in these mountains, rediscovered them in the headwaters of Birch and Trout creeks on the reservation.

That was in 1974. Don enlisted the help of fellow Trout Unlimited member Buck Douglass, whose ranch ambles along the eastern slope of the Deep Creek Mountains. Highly respected by the Goshutes, Douglass helped Don and the Great Basin Chapter of TU develop a partnership to fence cattle out of the creeks on the reservation. Douglass developed brood ponds to raise Bonneville cutts on his own ranch, mostly at his own expense. Together, they made incubators from abandoned refrigerators placed on the ground next to a spring creek. Water from the creek was piped into the top, passed over the eggs, and flowed out another pipe at the bottom. When the eggs hatched, and the fry matured to fingerling size, they swam down the outflow and into the stream. Cheap and effective, the method worked. As the Bonneville cutts grew in the streams and brood ponds, Don, Douglass, and tribal leaders such as Milton Hooper noticed that the flanks of these trout bore a more intense shade of vermillion than any other cutthroats. *Ainka painkwi* had returned! Now, nearly thirty-five years after those first fragile populations were re-discovered, "red trout" have been re-established in eleven streams on the reservation.

Bonneville cutthroats aren't the only trout making a recovery in this high arid country. Lahontans, the leviathans of the cutthroat tribe, are also reestablishing themselves. Journals of immigrants headed to California in the 1840s reported plentiful trout with large black spots taken from the Humboldt River. While these never reached the size of the mammoth sixty-pound Lahontans harvested commercially from Pyramid Lake north of Reno, six- to twelve-pound fish were not uncommon in the Humboldt and its tributaries.

Like the Bonneville cutts, the Lahontans found in the rivers of this high desert are refugees from another huge 8,500-square-mile ice-age lake that filled the basins of western Nevada from the Idaho line southwest to California. By the 1900s large Lahontans were largely gone from tributaries to the lake of the same name. Perhaps the last really big one, reports Pat Coffin, fisher-

TU in Action

The low-cost high-results restoration of Bonneville cutthroats in eleven creeks in the Goshutes Reservation returned "red trout" to their native waters and will provide the Goshute tribe with an economic resource.

Fencing out cattle was a crucial component of the Goshutes and Marys River projects, where 128 miles of stream are now open to public angling.

Both projects inspired additional work with Bonneville cutts including Warren Colyer's tracking of migration patterns of the species in the Bear River (Idaho, Utah, Wyoming) using implanted transponders the size of a grain of rice.

ies biologist with the Bureau of Land Management, was inadvertently taken in 1972 by an angler who had paused to sit and rest for a while on a beaver dam high in the Marys River drainage. His fly was dangling in the water behind him. It was snatched by what proved to be a twenty-five-inch Lahontan.

Pat, like Don, has spent decades restoring habitat so that the cutthroats he loves can regain their native headwaters. His work got a boost in 1988 when the Nevada Council of Trout Unlimited stepped up to the plate. Then–Council President Matt Holford and a coalition of organizations including the B.L.M., Nevada Division of Wildlife, the U.S. Forest Service, the U.S. Fish and Wild Life Service, a number of ranchers such as the Gibbs and Wright families, and sportsmen raised $180,000. Included in that sum was a $45,000 grant from Barrick Goldstrike Mines, Inc., major landowners in the watershed. These funds, reported Jason Dunham in his 1998 article for *Trout Magazine*, initiated a series of land swaps and conservation easements that opened 128 miles of the Marys to recreational angling, provided money for fencing to protect the streams from cattle, allowed removal of culverts and construction of new bridges, and supported scientific studies. Change comes slowly and for every creek where cutts are being re-established, there are ten that need help. Dedicated champions like Don Duff and Pat Coffin are in their sixties now and still hard at it. Their successes have come through partnerships with tribes, public agencies, private corporations, and volunteer groups. Such partnerships, like habitat, require informed stewardship. The question now is this: Who will carry on Don's and Pat's work for the next generation?

Managing water flows, fencing out cattle, and replanting riparian buffers have returned cutthroats to their native range. (above)

How's the Fishing?

Fans of native trout will enjoy adding Lahontans and Bonnevilles to their life lists. This is the best place I know to use a 3-weight as an excuse to escape the interstate and cut across the high desert shared by Utah and Nevada. Check in at the tribal office at the Goshutes Reservation south of Wendover and ask about fishing Trout and Birch Creeks or the ponds at Fish Springs. More adventurous anglers will pick up copies of the Double Mountain and Jarbridge 1:100,000 scale maps and carefully follow dirt roads to the campsite at the base of the Jarbridge Wilderness. Hike upstream. Fish the pools in June. Any #12 to #16 attractor or nymph will do nicely.

CHAPTER 8

Deschutes River, Oregon

The largest Pacific salmon has many names. Off the sand-bars at the mouth of the Campbell River in British Co-lumbia, where Roderick Haig-Brown wrote his books, it's the Tyee. Alaskans call it king. In Oregon and the Pacific Northwest, it's the chinook, named, like the warm mountain winds, for the tribe that lived north of the Columbia River. German naturalist Johann Julius Walbaum was the first to describe them scientifically in 1792. He named them *Oncorhynchus tshawytscha*, onkos meaning "hook" and rynchos for "nose." *Thawytscha* is the local name for the fish on Kamchatka where he discovered it. Walbaum apparently got around. Among other species credited to him are the great barracuda and the sheepshead.

The Columbia and its tributary from the south, the Deschutes, boast two chinook popula-tions. Fall chinooks, which return from late summer through early winter, tend to dig their redds in the main stream, lower in the drainage. Spring chinooks, on the other hand, enter fresh wa-

A historic highway for spawning chinook salmon and steelhead, the Deschutes was blocked by two dams.

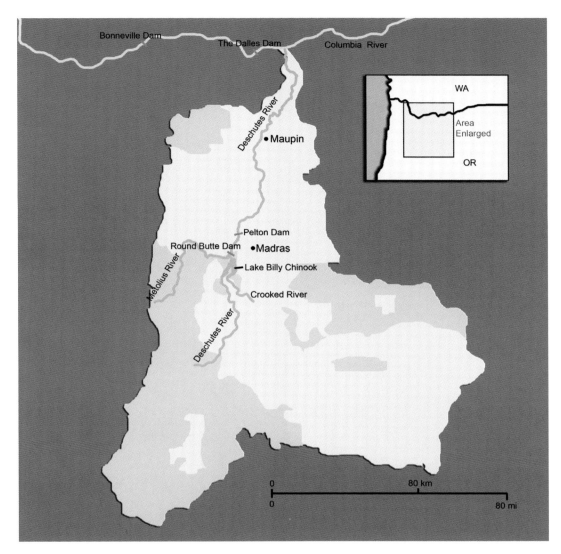

ter just before summer. They hole up in cold pools in tributary headwaters until they spawn and die during fall. While the progeny of fall chinooks make a dash for the ocean within months of emerging from their redds, the salmon of spring spend more than a year in their natal streams before heading to the ocean. Autumn chinooks average half again as large as their springtime cousins because they spend more time at sea.

Both types of chinooks once enjoyed free spawning runs up the Columbia and many of its tributaries until the Rock Island Dam, 453 miles upstream from the river's mouth, was sealed in 1932. The first of the Columbia's behemoth barriers, Bonneville Dam, 40 miles upstream from Portland and 146 miles from the ocean, was closed in 1938. Not twenty years later a second main river dam, this one at The Dalles just downstream from the mouth of the Deschutes, was finished. Though Bonneville and The Dalles dams each contain a stair-step set of artificial pools and falls to allow fish passage up the river and a passage for them to come back down, most salmon didn't use them. The chinooks were, and still are, effectively barred from spawning in the Columbia's watershed of 143 million acres, an area about the size of France.

Migrating chinook and steelhead that do manage to struggle their way past the Bonneville and The Dalles dams, turn south into the Deschutes and eventually run into Portland General Electric's Pelton Dam 100 miles upstream. Built in 1957, it impounds seven-and-a-half miles of the Deschutes. When plans for Pelton first became public in 1949, Native Americans and anglers, alarmed by the reduced runs of salmon attributable to dams on the Columbia, mounted fierce opposition. They feared that the dam would further reduce the chinook spawning runs. They also worried that since Pelton was to be a peak power facility, generating only during periods of high demand, the flows would either flood or trickle.

In response to these complaints, Portland General Electric (PGE) added a three-mile-long fishway and a regulating dam to even out Pelton's water releases. Though salmon and steelhead turned up their snouts at the fish passage, the regulating dam made flows from power generation more consistent. Seven years after that a second dam, Round Butte, was completed roughly eight miles upstream from Pelton. Four hundred and forty feet tall, Round Butte was more than twice as high as its downstream sibling. An aerial tram carried trapped adult salmon up and over the dam. A "skimmer" allowed smolts, like kids in a water slide, to ride a current of water in a pipe over and down the face of the dam. Rube Goldberg would have loved it.

The problem was that the salmon did not. Spawning returns continued to decline. The water temperatures in Lake Billy chinook upstream from Round Butte proved to be a big problem. You see, cold water is heavier than warm water. Cool flows from a tributary, the Metolius, sank under those from the Crooked River and the upper Deschutes, both warmer bodies of water. Spring salmon, looking to spawn in the cold Metolius, had a hard time finding it. Returning smolts, riding the river's currents back toward the dam and, eventually, the sea, got lost in swirling warm eddies from the other tributaries.

Layers of basalt cover porous aquifers that seep snowmelt from decades past into the Deschutes, augmenting with more cold water releases from Round Butte and Pelton Dams. (left)

As part of the Federal Energy Regulatory Commission's (FERC) relicensing of the Pelton-Round Butte dams in 2004, PGE and the Confederated Tribes of the Warm Springs Reservation—which owns one-third of the hydro complex—agreed to construct a 270-foot-tall water intake tower. Instead of coming only from the bottom of the lake, water for generation will now be primarily drawn from the top of the tower during the downstream migration period for spring salmon. Downstream, the river will warm slightly in the spring, providing better habitat for young fall chinook, steelhead, and the ubiquitous redband rainbows. During summer and early fall, which can be scorching here in central Oregon, the tower will draw more water from the bottom of the lake to cool the river.

The top of the tower resembles a huge garage turned upside down. Salmon migrating toward the sea will be drawn into large rectangular screened openings that wedge down to huge vertical "vees," where the fish will be trapped, transported by truck to below the regulating dam, and released. The intake floats and rides up and down with the level of the lake on a long tube-like conduit that slides into a collar anchored over the main intake near the base of the dam. The tube is forty feet in diameter, and is flexible enough to withstand high wind-driven waves and possible earthquake tremors. To be operational by 2009 and resembling something out of *Star Wars*, the combined intake and fish passage tower should reopen 226 miles of potential upstream spawning habitat at a cost of $62 million to PGE and the Confederated Tribes.

TU in Action

Provided expertise and leadership in renegotiation of the FERC license for Pelton-Round Butte hydrosystem.

Outcomes included a new 270-foot water intake tower that will enhance spawning opportunities for wild spring chinooks. Its $62 million cost is being funded by PGE and the Confederated Tribes.

How's the Fishing? An easy shot from Portland, portions of the Deschutes are fishable year-round. Salmon and steelhead fishing is a matter of skating

bombers or other riffle-hitched ties, or swinging traditional sparse salmon patterns gently over each rock in every run. Though floating is the best way to cover the river, you'll be wading whenever you cast, as fishing from boats is prohibited. This is 8-weight country. Intermediate sinking lines and shooting heads are not out of place. Be sure to fish with a buddy. Not only is the current heavy, but encounters with rattlesnakes are not infrequent.

Mike Beagle

Spring and fall runs of chinook, steelhead, and redband trout try the drags of anglers' reels. (left)

Mike Beagle

In the shank of a hot summer's day, fog settles on the Deschutes.

The drift boats are gone, and all of the river you can see is yours.

CHAPTER 9

Falling Spring, Pennsylvania

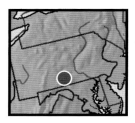 From Antrim, Ireland, the four Chambers brothers—James, Robert, Joseph, and Benjamin— immigrated to the colonies in 1730. Farmers, they sought rich soil and, just as important, water of the highest quality. They made their way to Fishing Creek west of the Susquehanna near the border of what would become Maryland, and eventually platted a farm and built a mill, both of which proved prosperous. But more and more people were streaming up the river from Chesapeake Bay every day, and the area soon became too crowed for the Chambers. They decided to push on inland.

Though their specific route is uncertain, it's likely that they followed the Susquehanna north to skirt South Mountain, the eastern rim of the limestone valley that runs south along the Appalachians all the way to Alabama. They probably entered the valley across from Harrisburg and followed Conodoguinet Creek south. James settled at the head of Great Spring, known today as Big Spring. Robert followed the Conodoguinet for another ten miles and laid claim to land around Middle Spring just northwest of Shippensburg. Joseph and Benjamin settled twelve miles on down the valley, where Falling Spring comes in to the Conococheague Creek. The settlement they founded would become Chambersburg in 1764.

There they erected a sawmill and, later, a flour mill, the first of five mills on the roughly five-mile-long creek. Because the gradient is fairly slight, only twenty-six feet per mile, each mill dam created a fairly lengthy and broad pond that filled with sediment as trees were cut for timber and fuel and the land was tilled. In 1792 another early miller, Jacob Stauffer, erected his wheel just east of where Interstate 81 crosses Falling Spring. Stauffer began to cultivate the stream's native watercress and sell it commercially.

Lurking in Stauffer's cress beds were native brook trout. They, or their descendants, still occupy the mileage immediately downstream from where the spring bubbles from the base of a wooded hillside. "They're there," says Mike Heck, president of Falling Springs TU, the chapter that for the past thirty years has been caretaker of Falling Spring. Brook trout also thrived, originally, in the other two famous Cumberland Valley spring runs. Theodore Gordon caught native brookies in Big Spring Creek when he fished it early in the 1900s. Visiting Brits wrote home about catching brook trout in the four-pound range in the 1920s. They're gone now, thanks to a stumble by the Pennsylvania Fish and Boat Commission. They opened a hatchery at the spring in 1973 and its effluent wiped out the remaining brookies along with the wild browns in the river. There is no doubt that big brookies also inhabited the nearby Letort before agriculture forever changed the character of that stream, and browns were introduced instead.

Great swirling clouds of *tricorythodes* drew George Harvey to Falling Spring in 1927. He sat in the grasses and watched these, among the tiniest of mayflies, emerge. He followed the flies' brief aerial dances over the riffles and saw them fall as spinners, triggering sips from multitudes of

PRIVATE PROPERTY
fly fishermen Only

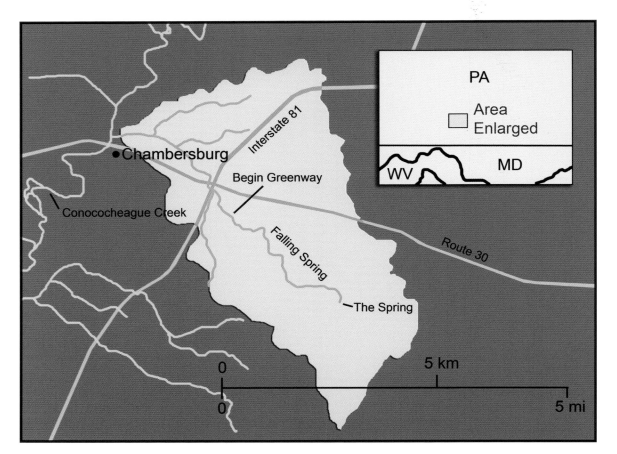

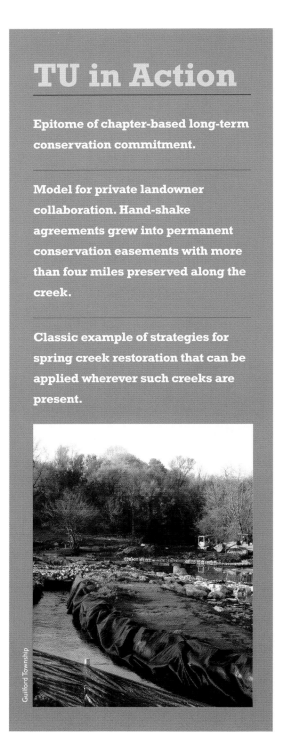

TU in Action

Epitome of chapter-based long-term conservation commitment.

Model for private landowner collaboration. Hand-shake agreements grew into permanent conservation easements with more than four miles preserved along the creek.

Classic example of strategies for spring creek restoration that can be applied wherever such creeks are present.

trout. By 1932 he had perfected his patterns and spread the word about Falling Spring. Reputed to have the best trico hatch in the East, the creek began to draw anglers from across the country, all addicted to catching large trout on No. 24 and 26 flies tied on tippets fine enough to thread the eyes of their hooks.

From Carlisle, forty miles north, the Letort's doyens Vince Marinaro and Charlie Fox cast their terrestrials over Falling Spring, experienced its tricos, and wrote about what they learned. When they fished the stream in the 1950s and 1960s, they found it severely degraded. According to a 1973 study, Falling Spring had the highest nitrate load of any spring creek in the Great Valley. The culprit was agriculture, an unintended consequence of stream-side grazing and intensive fertilization of row and fodder crops. As a youth, Mike Heck accompanied his dad on fishing outings on the creek and remembers seeing tricos swarming above the creek's riffles. When he became old enough to flyfish, he says that the trico clouds were just a memory.

Sediment from farming and from new home construction was choking the stream. Determined to do something about the problem, the Falling Springs Chapter of TU was created in the mid-1970s and initiated its first project—bank stabilization and tree plantings in 1977. To serve the new houses, a sewage line was inserted along Falling Spring and the creek was shunted out of the way. The raw scar healed, and the Pennsylvania Fish and Boat Commission tried a variety of stocking and regulation programs to restore the stream. None of them worked very well. Then, in 1988, a new subdivision was proposed at the headwaters. Two Maryland anglers, Dennis LaBare, a stream ecologist and TU member, and Bill Horn, former Assistant Secretary of the Interior for Fish, Wildlife and Parks, teamed up to see what could be done to protect Falling Spring. On a lovely spring day (of course), thirty TUers and other interested citizens met with Horn and La-Bare at a Chambersburg motel and Falling Spring Greenway, Inc., was created. Its mission was stewardship of the creek.

Guilford Township, through the jurisdiction of which Falling Spring flows, became actively involved in the early 1980s. As Greg Cook, chairman of the township's Board of Supervisors remem-

The public-private partnership restored flows of Falling Spring to its original channel. (above)

By 1932, George Harvey had pioneered trico patterns to match swarms of tricorythodes mayflies, the signature hatch of Falling Spring. (right)

Guilford Township requires conservation and public access easements for development along Falling Spring.

bers it, "TU came to us with a novel idea. They wanted to preserve something rather than develop it." That initial contact has flourished into a three-way partnership among the township, the Greenway, and Trout Unlimited. Early work by TU and the Greenway caused Pennsylvania's Department of Environmental Protection to request that the township amend its subdivision and land development ordinance to project Falling Spring. The township responded by requiring that new stream-side developments contain a seventy-five-foot conservation easement and a thirty-five-foot public access easement. Developers balked at first, but Cook, a township native committed to conservation, and his fellow supervisors emphasized the importance of preserving the stream.

The township, Greenway, and Fallings Spring chapter were joined at the hip. Together they work with landowners and local government to galvanize the funding and people power needed to rejuvenate the creek. The result has benefited all. Ecotone, a firm that specializes in environmental remediation, was hired to do the work and adopted Falling Spring as a demonstration project. With state grants, the firm provides stream design and the heavy equipment necessary to put in place the heavy rock and structures imitating undercut banks that narrow the channel, remove sediment from increased flows, and provide shelter for trout. Valley Quarries contributed rock for the project. Guilford Township, for which Heck works, provides a free office for the chapter and allows him occasional use of backhoes for stream-related projects. Over the past twenty years, the coalition has generated more than $1 million for work on Falling Spring, renovated more than four miles of spring creek into a first class fishery, and opened it to public access. Just as important, the tricos are beginning to swarm again.

Luca Adelfio

How's the Fishing?

On the bucolic meadows here, the chance of tagging a rainbow of twenty inches or more are better than you'd ever imagine. That's what produces those looks of wonder on the faces of anglers who stare at their snapped 7X tippets. Go fine, use finesse, and fish well all year. Parking areas are scattered conveniently along the stream. Pick an empty one and go to work.

CHAPTER 10

Garcia River, California

In 1950, when she was newly wed, Bonny Jean Morgan and her husband moved from Pennsylvania to Point Arena, California. He, a diesel mechanic, found steady work repairing engines on fishing boats and heavy equipment used for logging. Three children were born to the couple. "We fished every weekend," she said, sitting in front of her garage with her neighbor, Mary, shelling peas one recent sunny July afternoon. The boys would bring home cutthroats from the creek that flowed through the town into the Pacific, where the salmon boats dock. "Sometimes they were big," she remembers, but most often a foot or so in length.

One of the family's favorite getaways was Ten Mile River, about fifty miles north along one of the most stunning coastlines in North America. Here the Pacific, its broad beds of kelp heaving in the swells, crashes against cliffs rising from the sea. Fountains of spume jet into the air. Rafts of sea lions float off their rookeries on rocky isles. Petrels wheel overhead. Wings spread, cormorants bask in the sun. The bench above the cliffs is broad and colored like the coat of a lion. In

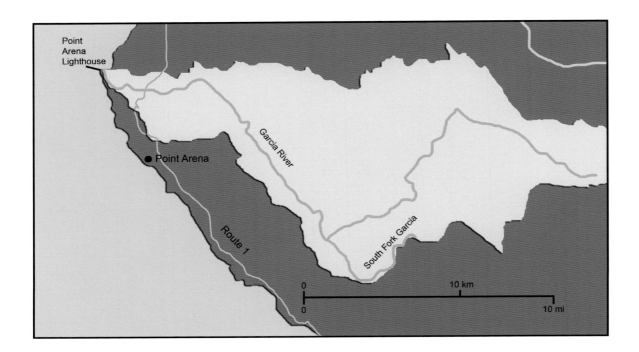

summer, the Morgan family camped on Ten Mile. Come winter, they'd make the drive for runs of coho and steelhead.

Those runs are vastly reduced from the Morgans's days. In the 1940s, more than 400,000 coho returned to spawn in their natal streams. Now the number is closer to 10,000. The story is similar with steelhead, those creek-bred rainbows that flee to salt, get fat, and return to spawn and bust the tackle of the untutored. Though no one is quite sure about the effects of shifting currents due to climate-induced changes in sea temperature, everybody agrees that degradation of habitat from outmoded agricultural, logging, mining, and development practices as well as overfishing by commercial interests has taken a huge toll.

It's like everywhere: Nevada, Montana, Virginia, you name the state. Allow cattle free access to a creek and their hooves will cleave a streambank with every step. They'll grind the soil, whatever its composition, into a morass. The vegetation they don't eat will be trampled and killed. When a stream that's been beaten down by cows floods, the channel spreads and shallows. Sediment is picked up and flushed downriver, filling pools and choking spawning redds.

Sediment is a byproduct of logging as well. Even if the timber is harvested selectively, roads cut into the sides of the mountains and yards carved into slopes so logs can be gathered and loaded onto trucks leave raw scars. These scars, in turn, bleed sediment—particles as small as grains of sand to dime-size pieces of gravel. Among the biggest sources of sediment are old logging tracts.

Mendocino County is known for its abundant stands of Douglas fir and redwood. There's something in a redwood's genes that makes it point straight to the heavens, almost no matter what. Should a violent storm off the Pacific fell a redwood, each of its branches will do its best to climb toward the noonday sun. Occasionally you'll see redwoods growing in a row as straight as if planted by a German forest meister. You won't lose much money if you bet that they're sprouts from a fallen tree. Circular stands grow from old stumps, which are often left by loggers precisely for that purpose. Only twenty percent of new redwoods come from seeds. Young trees, if the fogs and rainfall cooperate, can grow as much as three feet a year. Like all of us, they slow down as they get older.

In 1998, Mendocino Redwood Company (MRC) acquired about 350 square miles, roughly 228,800 acres, in Mendocino and Sonoma counties. The Garcia flows through its southernmost tract. Abused by years of shortsighted management and by clear-cutting and burning, MRC's acreage bore heavy stands of scrub tan oak, an interesting tree with little commercial value that

flowers like a chestnut, grows acorns like an oak, and keeps its leaves like an evergreen. No bones about it, MRC is in business to make money. It's the sole supplier of redwood to Home Depot. It thinks of its forests as an industrial resource.

For years, the previous owner had ignored entreaties by local commercial fisherman and logger turned conservationist, Craig Bell, and the Garcia River Watershed Advisory Group which he headed. When MRC acquired much of the Garcia's South Fork watershed, Bell turned to Steve Trafton, then TU's California coordinator. Trafton had a plan: storm-proof logging roads that ribbon MRC's holdings. Active roads should be regraded to spill water gently. Abandoned roads should be reseeded. Culverts should be steeply angled approximating the natural slope of the land. And where possible logs should be transferred from where they're cut to yards where they're loaded onto trucks by aerial cable, rather than being dragged by skidders down the mountainsides.

In MRC president Sandy Dean and the Donald Fisher family (who own MRC, as well as the Gap), Bell and Trafton found receptive ears. Ditto in Russ Shively, MRC forest manager. Originally from Ohio, he has worked in this forest for thirty years. Following advice from TU, consultants, and his own considerable common sense, he captained the restoration effort. He takes pride in it. So do MRC's employees and subcontractors who hunt and fish. They need their jobs, of course, but they want deer and coho and steelhead too. MRC's enlightened approach delivers the promise of both.

The work, which began in 1998, continues. Thousands of tons of sediment have been prevented from entering the Garcia. Downstream, near the mouth of the river, Bell has just completed bank stabilization on Stornetta Farm. Owners fenced out cattle. Bell and TU work crews installed willow mats, log deflectors, and root wads to force the Garcia back into its historic channel. Improved velocity has flushed sediment from spawning beds. Walking the banks, you can now see juvenile steelhead of six to ten inches darting in and out of brushy root wads. Bell will tell you, with the excitement of a boy expecting a pony for Christmas, of the redds of pink salmon he spotted just downstream of the bridge where Route 1 crosses. Nobody can even remember when pink salmon last used the Garcia to spawn.

On the Garcia, Mendocino Redwood Company and TU developed techniques to mitigate sedimentation from logging roads.

Russ Schnitzer

How's the Fishing? Coho are an endangered species along the California coast and may not be taken, but the Garcia offers a good fishery for winter steelhead. The season runs from November through March, and, as of this writing, regulations permit one steelhead per day taken with barbless hooks.

Great Smoky Mountains, North Carolina and Tennesee

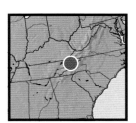 There's no telling how long speckled trout have lived in the Great Smoky Mountains. Some say they've been there for more than a million years. Steve Moore, who has studied them for the past three decades, figures they've been around for 15,000 years, ever since the last time glaciers pushed south. "Specks" is what southern mountaineers called them, but Moore, the chief fisheries biologist in the Great Smokies, knows them as brook trout—*Salvelinas fontinalis*—one of two freshwater salmonids native to the eastern United States. The other, *Salvelinas namaycush* or lake trout, is the most widely distributed salmonid in North America and found throughout the Great Lakes watershed and most of Canada. Neither is a trout. Both are char.

In the United States, brookies are by far the more widely distributed of the two. Their range cuts across our northern tier all the way to the headwaters of the Mississippi River and juts down along the spine of the Appalachians almost as far south as Atlanta. Ubiquitous in eastern boreal

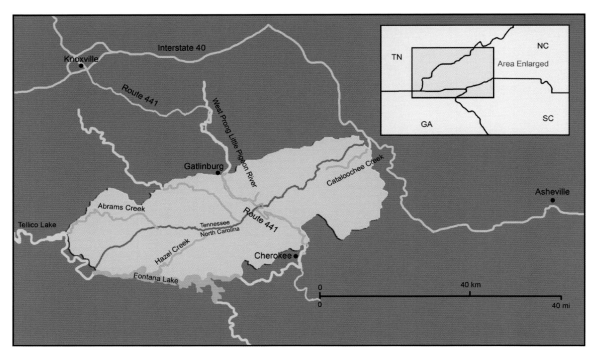

Canada, brookies found shelter in the Great Smokies when the valley streams that they'd once inhabited warmed with the climate.

The Smokies are the oldest and highest mountain range east of the Rockies. Their quartzites, phyllites, slates, and schists were formed 540 million to a billion years ago and are extremely resistant to weathering. Wisped with tendrils of haze that led the Cherokee to call the mountains *Sha-co-na-qe*, the place of blue smoke, the peaks get about eighty-five inches of rainfall each year. That's about one inch every four days.

Isolated by its climate and jagged high terrain, the Smokies have attracted other boreal fugitives as well—Frasier firs and red spruce, juncos and red squirrels, and dainty bluets that burst forth after snowmelt. On the spray cliffs of scattered southwest-facing cliffs laced with waterfalls, you'll also find an array of ferns, mosses, and liverworts native to the tropics, evidence of a time when continental drift positioned the Smokies much closer to the Equator.

Invasion of the mountains by white settlers came close to wiping out native brookies. Along with grits, fat back, and molasses, specks were common fare on mountaineer tables. One enterprising chap, Turkey George, once paid his dentist bill with 200 brook trout! Logging denuded steep hillsides. Streams were dammed. Resulting ponds were filled with floating logs. Then the loggers blew up the dams, causing a tsunami of water and tumbling poplar, fir, and hemlock butts to flood down the narrow mountain gorges, scouring streambeds clean as a hound's teeth. Down barren slopes washed tons of sediment that smothered breeding sites for fish and aquatic insects. Unshaded and choked with silt, mountain streams offered little better habitat than the warm turbid valley waters that the brookies had fled in the first place.

Unlike the leviathans of Labrador or the three- and four-pounders of Maine, brook trout of the southern mountains never grew very big. A foot-long brookie was cause for comment; most averaged six inches. Dissatisfied with the puny little brookies, the logging magnates imported rainbows. More aggressive than brook trout, the rainbows grew faster and bigger. Who cared? A trout was a trout, wasn't it?

The plundering of the Great Smokies appalled many, including an influential couple, Mr. and Mrs. Willis P. Davis, from nearby Knoxville. Returning from a visit to national parks in the West, they wondered aloud in 1923, "Why can't we have a national park in the Smokies?" The movement caught hold, Congress passed a bill authorizing the creation of the park in 1926, John D. Rockefeller, Jr., gave $5 million to buy land (matched with funds from North Carolina and

Wispy tendrils of haze led the Cherokee to call the mountains *Sha-co-na-qe*, the place of blue smoke.

"Specks" were a staple of the mountaineer's diet until these brook trout were all but wiped out by logging. Among the first priorities of the new national park: restore trout fishing to entice traveling anglers. (right)

Pattersonville / Dreamstime

TU in Action

The Little River Chapter of Trout Unlimited was formed to assist the park in monitoring water quality, conducting research, cleaning up streams, and providing additional funding for special projects.

Along with the neighboring Great Smoky Mountains Chapter in nearby Knoxville, the Little River Chapter has contributed more than 120,000 hours of volunteer labor and been influential in raising nearly $2 million for brook trout restoration.

Identification of Southern Appalachian Brook Trout fostered creation of the Eastern Brook Trout Joint Venture which unites seventeen states with federal and state agencies in the restoration of brookies from Maine to Georgia— the largest conservation effort in TU history.

Tennessee), and the park's first superintendent and seven rangers were hired in 1931. By then the brookies were in sad shape. Moore estimates that from 1900 to when the first rangers reported for duty, the park had lost half of its original population of brook trout.

High on the park's list of priorities was attracting tourists. Fishing could be a major draw. Among the first of the park projects was construction of fish-rearing ponds along the headwaters of the Little Pigeon at Chimney Campground on the Tennessee side. In his monthly report for April 1935, Park Superintendent J. Ross Eakin stated that 80,000 rainbow and 40,000 brook trout had been placed in the ponds.

Proud of his success, Eakin modestly enthused: "Fishing season in part of our streams opened on April 16. Many people have caught the daily limit of 10 trout 10 inches long or better. Local papers have commented upon the improved fishing." It didn't take long—only fifteen years—for the park to stop stocking brook trout. It was a no-brainer: The outdoor press was full of yarns about robust rainbows being pulled from Western waters. Why not offer even more of them up here in the Great Smokies? Turned out to be the right decision, though for a completely wrong reason.

Sometime in the mid-1970s, Mark Stoneking was studying brook trout at Penn State. He contacted the park and asked for some Smoky Mountain brookies. The fish were duly shipped, and

Each riffle and rock provides cover for hardy brook trout. (upper left)

Here in the Smokies, a distinctly southern brook trout was discovered by Steve Moore and his colleagues.

back came the report: The genetics of the park's brook trout did not resemble the others from the Northeast. Park biologists didn't know quite what to make of that. Pursuing the matter further, they hired a couple of graduate students, sampled a number of streams known to hold brookies, studied the fish, and found little evidence of any genetic uniqueness.

Despite the conflicting evidence, park biologists were concerned about the loss of brook trout habitat to rainbows, and stocking of the latter was stopped in 1975. Accelerating their worry was mounting evidence that acid rain, fogs, and snow was lowering the pH of headwaters. Smoky Mountain brookies, whatever their lineage, were being driven down from the headwaters by acidification and up by pressure from voracious 'bows.

The situation remained in limbo until a bulb went on in Moore's fertile mind. He dusted off the old files showing where brookies and rainbows had been planted and, lo and behold, the fish sent to Stoneking had come from one of six headwaters that the park had not stocked, while the grad students had sampled streams where brook trout had been planted. A second study of the Smokies' brook trout, completed in the late 1980s, confirmed that the park held a distinctly Southern Appalachian brook trout.

Small populations had survived in some of the park's most isolated headwaters: Bunches, Upper Raven, Hazel, Deep, and Eagle creeks; and some of the feeders to Cataloochee Creek—all on the North Carolina side of the park. In the 1990s, streams with barrier falls high enough to segregate brookies from downstream rainbows were identified. When removal of rainbows and browns above the barriers via electro-fishing proved ineffective, Moore and his colleagues turned to antimycin, an antibiotic that kills fish but not other aquatic life.

Heavy, public outcry became muted when Trout Unlimited and other conservation organizations endorsed the controlled use of antimycin. As this is being written, eleven brook trout streams totaling seventeen miles have been restored with Southern Appalachian-strain brook trout. Brookies are now legal quarry in all but three streams in the park.

Perhaps the greatest impact has been public awareness of brook trout as the primary native salmonid in the East. Beginning with a TU campaign in North Carolina and Tennessee dubbed "Back the Brookie," interest in restoration of brook trout has spread up the Appalachians all the way into Maine and resulted in the Eastern Brook Trout Joint Venture—a seventeen-state collaboration with six federal agencies, a number of universities, and TU councils and chapters representing more than half of TU's members committed to protecting brook trout habitat and their restoration. To date more than $1 million has been expended in the conservation of the East's most prevalent native salmonid.

Matt Handy

How's the Fishing?
The cessation of stocking in 1975 transformed what had primarily been a put-and-take fishery into one dominated by wild trout. Their size can be surprising, especially on creeks such as Hazel, Forney, Deep, and Eagle, which connect to Fontana Lake on the North Carolina side. If you want big fish, go to Alaska. Here, angling finesse with 4-weight systems with flies that match hatches of mayflies and caddis will result in success. Access is as easy as you like; it all depends on how far from your car you want to walk.

CHAPTER 12

Guadalupe River, Texas

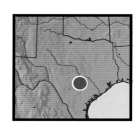 When ballots nominating candidates for inclusion in the revised edition of *TU Guide to America's 100 Best Trout Streams* began to come in, the names were mostly what you would expect: Henry's Fork, Madison, Au Sable, Beaverkill, you know the list. But among them was one river that was way off my radar, the Guadalupe, between Austin and San Antonio in Texas. I wasn't familiar with it. Bass and catfish water, maybe? One of the 100 best trout streams in America? This I had to see.

I packed a bag, boarded a flight, picked up a rental car in San Antonio, and met Mick McCorcle, then president of the Guadalupe River Chapter of Trout Unlimited, and a bunch of their members at the Grist Mill Restaurant next to Gruene Hall, the oldest dance palace in Texas. Country music fans will know that that's where George Strait earned his spurs. Over slabs of ribs and steak and bottles of Lone Star beer, they told how the Guadalupe became the best little trout stream in Texas.

Actually, there's more than one trout river in Texas. Each winter the state's Parks and Wildlife Department (TPWD) stocks more than 280,000 rainbows in the Brazos forks of the Trinity River near Fort Worth, and numerous community lakes around the state. There's also a small

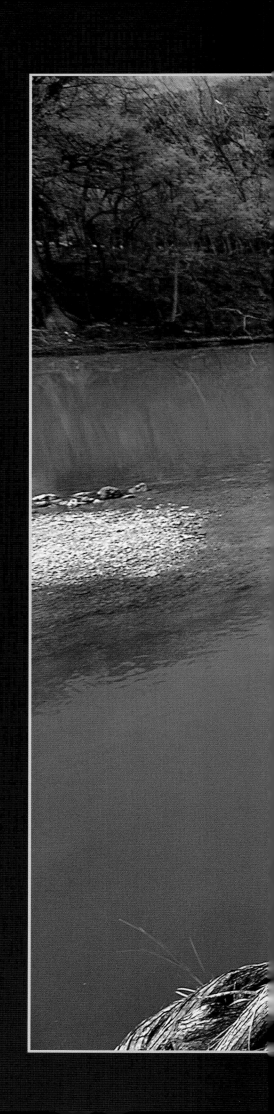

population of wild rainbows in McKittrick Canyon in Guadalupe Mountains National Park, though fishing for these is prohibited.

Lone Star beer more than lubricated the evening. It turned out that the brewery was partially responsible for Guadalupe making the 100 Best. About fifteen miles upstream from Gruene, Canyon Lake was impounded by the U.S. Army Corps of Engineers in 1964 to control the horrendous flooding generated by tropical storms that swing inland and then stall over the Texas Hill Country. As the lake was filling in 1966, folks decided it'd be cool to hold a boat show. A group of trout anglers, a fellow named Bill Pabst among them, thought it'd be fun to have a trout tank where kids could catch rainbows. Lone Star brewery agreed and made it happen. When the picnic was over, a few fish were left in the tank. It made sense to dump them in the river, no? So was born one of America's 100 Best Trout Streams.

The planners of the reservoir had known, of course, that the temperature of the water coming out of the bottom of the dam would be significantly colder than that of the river upstream. And they'd discussed whether or not a sustainable trout fishery could be created. But it took a gang of TUers to get the ball rolling. They collaborated with TPWD and experimented with stocking browns, cutthroats, and rainbows in the river downstream of the dam. Cutthroats may have once been native to the west Texas mountains, but are not found within the state today, as far as is known. Neither they nor the browns adapted well to the Guadalupe, and the rainbows were iffy. When TPWD stocked a strain of rainbows bred from Missouri Ozark stock, however, they had surprising success. The fish held over from year to year.

Nothing in Texas is ever done in a small way. And every three or four years, one of those tropical depressions staggers to a halt over the Hill Country and it rains and rains and rains. Flooding killed ten teenagers in 1997, when forty inches of rain fell in two days. Five years later, two weeks of summer rain dropped more than thirty-five inches and raised water levels forty-three feet above flood stage. Not only does the Guadalupe get blown out, but its flows, like most Western waters, can also be preempted by the highest bidder and by developers needing to irrigate the burgeoning communities downstream. The river flows and fishes best when it's running between 100 and 500 cfs. In times past, flow has dropped to 25 cfs, barely enough water to dampen felt on wading boots.

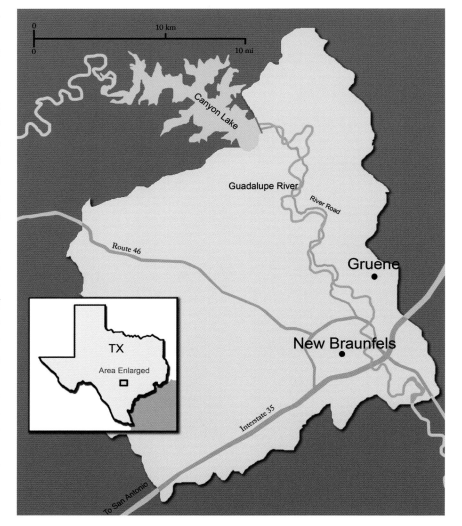

Spiking and falling flows certainly plague the rainbows, but the real challenge is maintaining water cool enough for a great enough distance below Canyon Dam to allow trout to survive the summer. Reducing summer flows to a trickle is sure death to rainbows attempting to make it through the blistering summer heat, to say nothing of leaving them with any energy to procreate. When flow regimen became an issue during an FERC license renewal in 2000, the Gua-

The river's huge rainbows rally TU's largest chapter—GRTU with its 4,000 members.

dalupe-Blanco River Authority said publicly that its planned sales of water and the maintenance of a full pool would have little or no impact on trout habitat. *Riiight*, thought Texas TUers. And one of them, David Schroeder, who'd been through water wars in Arkansas and Oklahoma, poked around and found a public notice inviting formal comment on the river authority's proposed license renewal and amendment to its release plan.

Prompt action by Schroeder and a few deep and savvy pockets among chapter members positioned the chapter to file a lawsuit with the Texas Natural Resource Conservation Commission requesting a "contested case hearing" of the water authority's plan. There's nothing Texans like better than a good scrap. TUers raised $100,000, went to court, and emerged with a double victory. The water authority, TU, and TPWD had to reach agreement on appropriate flows and, adding insult to injury, the water authority had to reimburse TU for its expenses because it had been less than accurate and forthcoming. The new agreement states that when the lake reaches full-pool, the authority has to maintain at least a flow of 200 cfs at the gauge downstream at Sattler from April through September. This, in effect, extends the range of trout habitat from five to ten miles below Canyon Dam.

The jury's still out on whether the Guadalupe can ever become a self-sustaining trout fishery. The river seems too prone to floods, like the one in 2002 when water roared eight feet over the spillway, sluiced tons of new gravel and silt into the river channel, and hung a school bus in a treetop. Such floods don't exactly help spawning. Still, there's no doubt that the Guadalupe is as viable a put-and-grow trout tailwater as any of those in the Southeast. And, the river has given trout anglers in Texas a rallying point. From sales of parking passes, the chapter maintains access corridors across private lands to the river. Funds raised augment stockings by TPWD of trout in the twelve- to twenty-four-inch range. Texas trouters, at least the 4,000 members of the Guadalupe River Chapter, the largest in Trout Unlimited, are justifiably proud of their only trout stream that holds fish year round. And as McCorcle didn't need to assure me at dinner that night, they sure know how to get out the vote.

TU in Action

The Guadalupe River Chapter of Trout Unlimited created and sustains the only put-and-grow public trout fishery in the Lone Star State.

It's the rallying point for 4,000 members who aren't shy about convincing the state legislature how it should vote on water issues.

Sale of parking permits along the river pays for stocking and provides funds supporting Trout in the Classroom, Project Kidfish, and the chapter's new Coldwater Outreach Conservation Fund that underwrites projects in other states.

How's the Fishing?

Wade or float the Guadalupe from November into April. It's a nympher's paradise. Fish bead-heads and brassies in sizes 16 and smaller beneath a strike indicator. No need to prove how far you can cast. Patience is more important, and the willingness to see a drift through from the moment the fly hits the water until it begins to swing in the current. The only warning you'll get of a strike will be a subtle twitch of your indicator. Raise your rod firmly but not too smartly lest you break your thin tippet. A stiffish nine-foot 5-weight rod works best.

Housatonic River, Connecticut

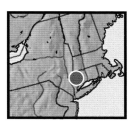
"There is no tonic like the Housatonic," boasts the Housatonic Fly Fishermen's Association. While attributed to poet and essayist Oliver Wendell Holmes, Sr., the saying likely didn't originate with him. As Holmes, co-founder of *The Atlantic Monthly*, said about another misquote: "I am afraid it does not belong to me, but I will treat it as I used to treat a stray boat which came through my meadow, floating down the Housatonic—get hold of it and draw it ashore, and hold on to it until the owner turns up."

In the 1840s, when Holmes was summering at his farm on the Housatonic south of Pittsfield, Massachusetts, the river was already deep in the throes of the Industrial Revolution. Dams were being put up wherever there was enough water to turn a wheel. In his 2004 book, *The Trout Pool Paradox*, George Black draws a compelling sketch of the history of the Housatonic:

"The wildest and most beautiful streams were precisely those that were used to generate the ugliest forms of industrial development and the worst kinds of environmental devastation. Few people remember any longer that the Housatonic Valley was the center of the U.S. iron and steel industry for a century before the Civil War."

Few know, either, that according to Black the Housatonic was the birthplace of America's vast network of hydro-electric plants. The first, near Canaan, opened in 1904. It generated electricity that was sold by the light bulb, and no bulb could burn before sundown or after the clock struck twelve. Next came Falls Village Dam, just 14 feet high, running 300 feet across the top of 50-foot-high Great Falls with the generators located below. Wires were strung to twelve towns. The dam backs up the Housy for 3.8 miles, a shallow and shadeless reservoir that captures heat like asphalt in August.

On some hot summer days, water released from the dam could exceed 80°F, lethal for trout. And since Northeast Utilities operated the generators for peak power, the Housy got one or two shots of hot water a day. Trout can adapt to changes in water temperature as long as they are not too often or too extreme. The Housy's were both. Fish kills were frequent in the 1980s and early 1990s, thanks to a nine-megawatt relic of the late Industrial Revolution.

Below Falls Village Dam, down a valley so beautifully bucolic that you'd never believe it cuts through the heart of the most intensely populated metropolitan corridor in the United States, flows twenty miles of the Housy, beloved by platoons of anglers from New York to Boston. According to Tim Barry, Connecticut's western district fisheries biologist, Atlantic salmon once spawned here. And before immigration of Europeans in the seventeenth and eighteenth centuries, brook trout were no doubt present. But at least since the 1940s, the river has been consistently stocked with rainbows, browns, and brookies, depending on the policies of the day. Today, browns are the featured species, though rainbows may be stocked again in the future. Trout grow fat on prolific hatches and swarms, now, of minnows and chubs.

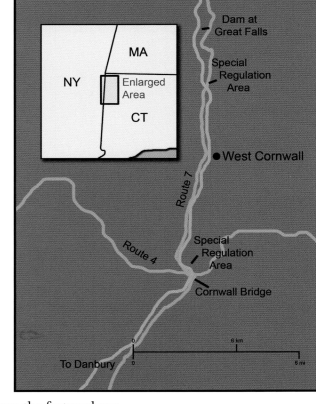

Housatonic River Outfitters

Wadable and fishable year 'round, the Housy's within easy casting distance of anglers from New York to Boston. (preceding page)

Hatches are prolific and hold-over trout become more finicky than you'd expect. (left)

Below Falls Village Dam, down a valley so beautifully
bucolic that you'd never believe it cuts through the heart of
the most intensely populated metropolitan corridor in the
United States, flows twenty miles of the Housy.

At least since the 1940s, the river has been consistently stocked with rainbows, browns, and brookies, depending on the policies of the day.

TU in Action

With thermometers taped to yardsticks, TU members and others gathered proof that hot peaking flows were cooking the Housy's trout.

TU partnered with Housatonic Fly Fishers Association to convince Federal Energy Regulatory Commission to force utility to require run-of-river flows.

It didn't take many trout floating belly-up to galvanize action among members of the Housatonic Fly Fishermen's Association (HFFA) and the nearby Naugatuck Chapter of TU. Learning in 1994 that Falls Village Dam would come up for relicensing in 2001, the vice president of TU's Naugatuck Chapter, Dan Kenny, wrote the Federal Energy Regulatory Commission (FERC) expressing extreme concern about the fish kills. HFFA, equally concerned, had been gathering water temperature data. With thermometers taped to yardsticks, they measured the differences between temperatures during releases and normal flow and found that releases were producing temperatures too hot for trout, even in thermal refuges.

FERC, as part of relicensing, required Northeast to conduct its own studies. There then began intense debate between the utility and FERC, which wanted the status quo, and TU and DEP whose analysis argued for run-of-river flows. FERC guru Mona Janopaul led TU's legal charge. As the arguments sharpened, more than a dozen stakeholders including the Housatonic Rainbow Club and Housatonic River Outfitters joined the coalition led by Kenny which now numbered more than 3,000. When Kenny changed jobs, Mike Piquette of HFFA took hold of the coalition's reins. By the time in 1999 when Northeast filed its application for relicensing, the utility and the coalition had reached agreement to operate the dam, and another one downstream at Bulls Bridge, for run-of-river flows. Essentially, "run-of-river" means flows that would occur naturally, given the amount of precipitation in the watershed.

The new regimen began in 2005. It took a year to work the bugs out of the system, and the first full year of natural flows didn't occur until 2006. Because of the annual instability of weather, five years will be required before the outcomes of run-of-river will be known. Preliminary observations suggest that the integrity of thermal refuges is more consistent, reports Barry. Reduced stress on the trout may enhance their ability to survive from one season to the next, but there's not enough data, yet, to tell. And while wild, stream-bred browns are occasionally found in the Housy, he is fairly certain they've moved into the river from tributaries. Why no significant reproduction in the river? It's just too hot, he explains, for sex.

Browns predominate, but anglers will find their share of 'bows too. (below)

Housatonic River Outfitters

How's the Fishing? A put-and-grow fishery with limited natural spawning, the Housy fishes best in spring and fall and, in summer, as early in the morning as you can see to cast a fly. A catch-and-keep river this is not. General Electric's manufacture of transformers at its massive plant in Pittsfield, not far from the farm where Holmes summered, added tons of PCBs to the Housy's sediments. A curse with a silver lining, the presence of PCBs led to the establishment of a trout management area that runs about ten miles from Rt. 112 in West Cornwall south to the bridge carrying Routes 4 and 7 across the river. Prolific hatches make for finicky fish. Check local flyshops for effective patterns.

CHAPTER 14

Kennebec River, Maine

Richard Procopio

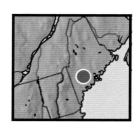

In bateaux hastily constructed of heavy green pine planks, Benedict Arnold and his troop of 1,100 American soldiers poled their way up the Kennebec and embarked on their ill-fated campaign to take Quebec from the British in the fall of 1775. Awkward as only an essentially flat-bottomed craft can be, especially when forced against the current, the bateaux demanded constant attention from the soldiers, leaving them scant time to admire the throngs of Atlantic salmon traveling with them upriver to spawn.

But they surely noticed massive pods of this greatest of all gamefish, so essential had Atlantic salmon been to the diets of Abnaki Indians and early whites who settled along the 150-mile-long river knifing through central Maine. By 1784, commercial fishing for salmon was going full throttle. That spring, a man named Rogers and six others reportedly harvested 9,000 salmon in gillnets off Hunnewell's Point at the mouth of the Kennebec. Three decades later, in 1818, the same location yielded only 1,134 salmon. Each fish averaged about twenty pounds and brought

about $1.00, or about $13.03 in 2006 dollars. Not much? Consider that $1.00 of the United States' total gross domestic product in 1813 is worth about $13,745 of ours today.

Salmon populations continued to plummet and people along the river who depended on their catch grew alarmed. In 1821 residents of Phippsburg petitioned Maine's state legislature to halt the construction of mill dams on the Kennebec because they disrupted the migration of salmon and alewives. These may have been the first American environmental activists. They, apparently, understood the dependence of a healthy economy on the natural environment. Their petition was summarily dismissed, as were those of other concerned parties in 1834. Plans to dam the Kennebec at Augusta moved into high gear.

The Kennebec River Dam Company completed the structure in 1837 and, to its credit, included a fish ladder. Unfortunately, a flood washed the ladder away the following spring. By the 1840s, the dam was powering seven sawmills, a grist mill, and a machine shop. Other dams followed, were blown out by hurricanes and ice jam floods, and were rebuilt longer and higher each time. The dam at Augusta was breached in 1846, 1855, and 1870. Its ownership was transferred in 1882 to the Edwards Manufacturing Company, which opened a knitting mill that employed more than 700 people. Electric generators were added in 1913. By then, salmon populations were little more than a memory.

Unionization of New England's knitting mills during the Great Depression accelerated the exodus of the region's industry to the Southeast. World War II and the Korean War, to lesser degree, spawned massive orders for cloth for blankets and uniforms and revived the river's mills, but only for a time. Rather than close, in 1973 Edwards sold its dam, mill, and name to Miller Industries. More than 800 jobs were saved, but only for a decade. The mill rolled its last bolt of fabric in 1983, and then 800 workers joined unemployment lines. In 1984 Edwards, salvaging what it could from what had become a financial albatross, signed a fifteen-year agreement to sell electricity for three times the going rate to Central Maine Power.

In the early 1980s, anglers began to push for the re-establishment of alewife runs in the Kennebec. They believed, and rightly so, that if alewives returned, so would saltwater striped bass and Atlantic salmon. In 1987, Maine's Department of Marine Resources started a campaign to restore the alewife migrations. The Kennebec Valley Chapter of Trout Unlimited championed the effort. Its members were among those who formed the Kennebec River Anglers Coalition in that same year; it eventually morphed into the Kennebec Coalition 1989.

After a full decade of work, the coalition and its partners—American Rivers, the Atlantic Salmon Federation, the Natural Resources Council of Maine, Trout Unlimited and its Kennebec Valley Chapter—were finally able to get approval to have the dam removed. The pivotal point came when TUers from the Kennebec chapter stayed late one night, pressing their case before the Federal Energy Regulatory Commission (FERC) examiners long after the high-priced power company consultants had gone home. Coming 165 years after its construction was first protested, elimination of the structure in the summer of 1999 became a model of collaboration, not just among conservation groups, but also by Florida Light and Power, which by then owned the structure, and Bath Iron Works, which provided funding.

Removal of Edwards Dam opened twenty miles of the Kennebec to runs of alewives, salmon, shad, and striped bass. An excellent brown trout tailwater fishery was the only casualty. When

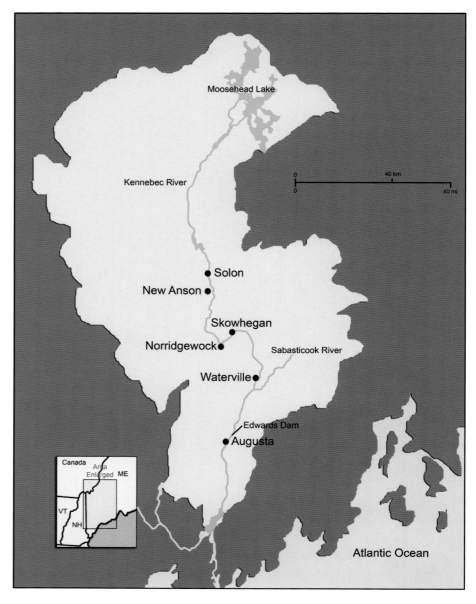

Removal of the Edwards Dam opened 20 miles of river to runs of alewives, Atlantic salmon, shad, and striped bass. (preceding page)

Richard Procopio

asked about how the river has changed since 1999, Mike Holt, owner of Fly Fishing Only, a shop on the river in Fairfield, will quip: "The guys who used to buy 6-weights for browns now buy 8-weights for stripers."

There's more too it, of course. A year after Edwards was taken out, a few Atlantic salmon spawned in the run of the river upstream. While lack of funding has prohibited an accurate survey of spawning redds in the Kennebec's main stem, the data that does exist suggests incremental annual increases. The Kennebec Valley Chapter of TU and other members of the coalition are hard at work on securing agreement of the FERC to deny the relicensing of Lockwood Dam nineteen miles above Edwards, and the Hydro-Kennebec Dam farther upstream. With support from the Maine Council of TU and TU's national staff, the Kennebec Valley Chapter has also been a partner in a string of legal court judgments against a small group of lakeside residents fighting the breaching of Fort Halifax dam on the Sebasticook. Freeing this river, which joins the Kennebec at Winslow, will open about 9,300 acres of river and tributary to recolonization by alewives, shad, salmon, and striped bass.

Richard Procopio

TU in Action

The Kennebec Chapter launches a historic campaign that raises $7.25 million in commitments from private industry to remove Edwards Dam and restore Kennebec River habitat.

Salmon, shad, striped bass, and alewives extend into spawning grounds last used in 1837.

Though it will be years before salmon recover, stripers and shad bring out anglers and their 8-weights. (left)

Russ Schnitzer

How's the Fishing? Angling for Atlantic salmon is prohibited. The catch-and-release season (artificial lures only) for striped bass runs from May 1 through June 30, and then opens to all tackle through the end of November. Fish from Fairfield down to Augusta. The best browns are found below Shawmut Dam and around Skowhegan and up to Madison, with the upper stretch offering the best wading. For rainbows, head north to Bingham and fish the Wyman Dam tailwater. But, the question is this: Why fish browns and 'bows in Maine when there are native populations of brookies and landlocked salmon? That's another story.

CHAPTER 15

Kettle Creek, Pennsylvania

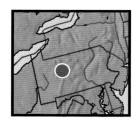 Near the rolling crest of the Alleghany Highlands in north-central Pennsylvania, where Two-mile Run gathers its water, spreads an open bald. The terrain wears a crew cut. Bristles of grass sprout from thin soil. Eventually, and it will be a long "eventually," the oaks and ash and poplar and shagbark hickory that once forested this strip-mined mountaintop will return. The coal is all but gone. If you listen, you can hear the wind in the grasses, the sound of the healing passage of time.

West of here, across Kettle Creek, the first coal strike was made in the early 1870s. The Kettle Creek Coal and Mining Company was hastily organized and built in the village of Bitumen, a dozen miles from the railroad town of Renovo. Local lore says the moniker stuck because the coal seam was discovered "by two men." The final spelling, however, is the same as the word for that acrid mix of flammable hydrocarbons found in coal and petroleum. Slovaks flocked to the region. Work, following the economic panic of 1873, was steady. Wages were good.

Life was also hard. Miners sank shafts through the nearly horizontal sandstones and shales much older than dinosaurs until they encountered a bed of coal, usually three to six feet in thickness. From there, they stoped their way through the coal—that is, they dug following the seam from its lowest elevation to its highest, so water that dripped from fractures and joints in the rock would run downhill, away from the face where they were mining and collect in the bottom of the shaft. Disasters, like the spark that set off the Cooks Creek explosion in 1888, which killed seventeen miners, were not uncommon.

Then, as now, Pennsylvania's coal miners formed a tightly knit community. When miner Mike Riczyk, who'd grown up in Bitumen, invited his friend Frank Klimkos and ten others from Indiana County to come to Cooks Creek for a bear hunt in the late 1930s, the men jumped at the chance. The gang took a bear and also developed a life-long love for the high plateau country, lush with swaths of laurel and deeply cut by narrow valleys that had streams full of trout. In 1940 Klimkos and his friends built a cabin on Cooks Run. After World War II he packed up his new wife and moved to nearby Renovo, where their first son was born.

Deep mining for coal is expensive, and the end of the war put the final nail in its coffin. A few small shafts continued to operate, but surface mining—which was cheaper and quicker—was taking over. Wagon drills bored holes in rock overlying coal seams. The holes were then charged with dynamite or other explosives, set off, and the shattered rock—called overburden—was loosened enough to be dumped down the nearest slope. Often containing tons of coal of such a poor grade as to have no commercial value, the overburden was aptly known as "spoil." With draglines and power shovels, Klimkos, stripped coal in open mines throughout the region. Little did he imagine that his second son, Mike, would later lead efforts to reclaim the mess left in strip mining's wake.

Mike was born in 1953, after Frank had moved his family back to Indiana County. Young Mike and his dad spent many weekends at the cabin on Cooks Run. There he learned to fish for brookies and stocked

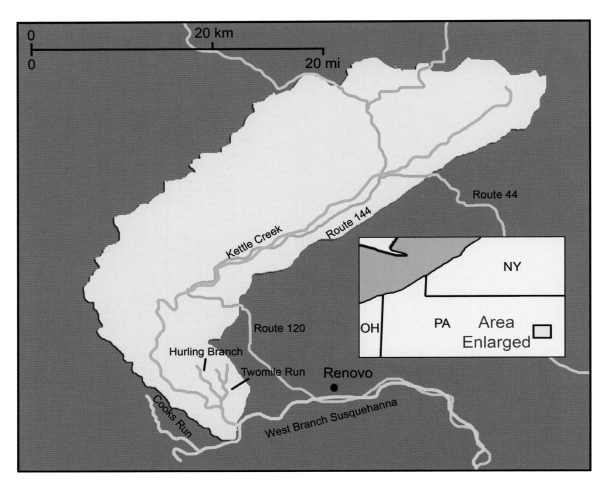

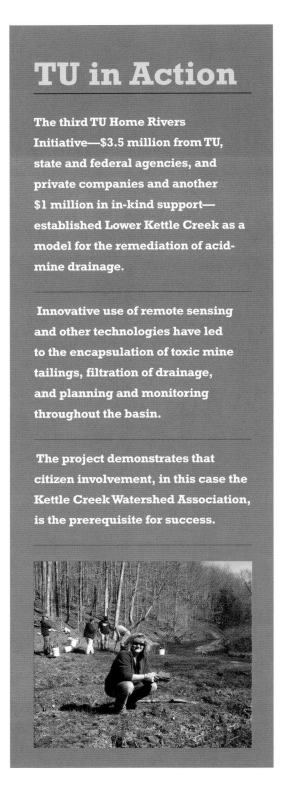

TU in Action

The third TU Home Rivers Initiative—$3.5 million from TU, state and federal agencies, and private companies and another $1 million in in-kind support—established Lower Kettle Creek as a model for the remediation of acid-mine drainage.

Innovative use of remote sensing and other technologies have led to the encapsulation of toxic mine tailings, filtration of drainage, and planning and monitoring throughout the basin.

The project demonstrates that citizen involvement, in this case the Kettle Creek Watershed Association, is the prerequisite for success.

rainbows and browns in the main stem of Kettle Creek. The year he turned nine, the U. S. Army Corps of Engineers completed the 165-foot-high Alvin R. Bush flood-control dam. Two-mile-long Kettle Creek Lake is prime smallmouth water, as are the eleven miles of water up to where Cross Fork comes in. Above that is trout country. For a mile below the dam, the Kettle Creek remains fishable. Then it drops into a seven-mile gorge.

In the gorge, Kettle Creek bangs its way around deep gray boulders, dashes through slick runs, lingers in deeply shaded pools, and gains speed again as the gradient drops. There has never been a more picturesque run of trout water. If you drive the road that runs along the creek as it descends the gorge, the one thing you notice is that there are no pullouts for anglers. Why? No trout or smallmouths are found here. The stream is all but dead, toxified by drainage from the coal mines that once operated in the highlands rising above this charming canyon.

Rock is seldom as solid as we'd like to think. Instead, it's riddled with fractures and joints. Gravity draws water—itself, a weak acid—down through the fissures. As it percolates through coal spoil, it dissolves the three metals primarily linked to acid mine drainage: aluminum, iron, and manganese. Pyrite, which we know as fool's gold but which is actually iron sulfide and which is usually present in strata that contain coal, reacts with ground water in the presence of oxygen to form sulfuric acid. Metals dissolved by acid mine drainage clog gills and suffocate fish. Increased acidity wipes out caddis, mayflies, and stoneflies, primary fodder for trout. No trout, not even brookies, the hardiest of the trout, can tolerate streams polluted by drainage that weeps from abandoned mines.

During his college years at Clarion State, Mike, Jr., continued fishing out of the cabin with his dad. The fishing, though, had turned sour. The acid-mine drainage had killed the trout and the fishing that he'd shared with Mike, Sr. In 1981, he took a job with the Bureau of Mining and Recreation. Why? "Hell, they polluted my favorite creek," he'll tell you, "and I wasn't about to let

Stained reddish orange, rocks where Kettle Creek dumps into the West Fork of the Susquehanna show the acid mine drainage. (top right)

Ponds were dug to filter out aluminum, iron, and manganese, the metals which suffocate fish and the insects on which they feed. (bottom right)

Amy Wolfe

Amy Wolfe

Amy Wolfe

them get away with that." For twenty-three years he worked for the Commonwealth, undoing the effects of coal mining. "Dad turned over Keating Mountain, Bitumen, and Twomile Run," he says, laughing. "I'm just trying to fix what he tore apart." He's had help from willing partners.

John Larson grew up in Emporium, about twenty-five miles northwest of Bitumen as the crow flies. He was among the founders of the Kettle Creek Watershed Association, which partnered with Trout Unlimited to create the Kettle Creek Home Rivers Initiative in 1998. Dean Mertz, who fished for brook trout in Twomile Run as a kid, and who wants his grandson, Josh, to have the same thrill, was another founder. That same year, Amy Wolfe (then Gottesfeld), a native of Bucks County who had recently graduated with a degree in environmental biology from Lock Haven University, was hired by TU to direct the Kettle Creek project. Lean and sharp as surgical steel, but softened with delightful humor, she became the Watershed Association's godmother.

Wolfe arranged the aircraft flights that collected infrared images she used to locate mine seeps. She set geophysical sensors to find pools of acid water hidden deep in abandoned mine shafts. She then forged a coalition of community residents, local industry, and state and federal agencies that eventually led to the clean-up of a fifty-seven-acre abandoned mine, the site of the grassy bald in Twomile Run's headwaters. She also helped develop a counter-intuitive remediation strategy—the use of mining to clean up mining—centered around the opening of old mines to remove high grade coal left as pillars and wall supports. Remining—economically feasible with today's high prices—in turn allows the old mines to be treated with anti-acid alkalines and then capped forever.

For this work, the Kettle Creek Watershed Association and Trout Unlimited were presented the Governor's Award for Watershed Stewardship in 2001. The project has now grown into a campaign to mitigate acid-mine drainage throughout the watershed of the West Branch of the Susquehanna, an area of 7,000 square miles. More than 300,000 gallons per minute of acid drainage flows into more than 1,100 miles of the river and its tributaries. Were it stopped, once-thriving coal towns such as Renovo, Westport, and Keating would see economic daylight again, brought this time by tourists from Pittsburgh and Philadelphia longing to get away to the Pennsylvania Wilds, to canoe and kayak these marvelously scenic rivers, to fish the mayfly hatches, and maybe to have a chance at a brookie that's found its way home.

With its prolific hatches, Kettle Creek is one of Pennsylvania's premier trout fisheries. (left)

Brookies are returning to Twomile Run, a tributary of Kettle Creek. (below)

Brent Golladay

How's the Fishing?

A put-and-grow stream with plenty of holdovers, Kettle Creek from the top of the lake on upstream is prime fly fishing water. If you can only use one pattern, it should be a tan caddis, but the sulphur hatch can be phenomenal. If you like to fish for wild brookies, you'll find them in most every tributary above the lake and in the river's headwaters near Oleona and Germania. A 3-weight is perfect.

CHAPTER 16

Kickapoo River, Wisconsin

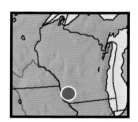 Toward the end of his foreshortened life, Roger Widner took to sitting on a grassy knoll where he could gaze southwest over the valley of the West Fork of the Kickapoo River. Before the maples and cottonwoods were leafed in full, he could see the new tin roof of the old school in Avalanche into which his parents had moved when he was three. He lived there still with his wife, Laurie, and their two kids. They sold beer, groceries, and trout flies in the rooms where his mother, Mary, had once taught children their ABCs.

From where he sat, he could also see the river. A placid stream with few riffles, it eases its way between banks of sand and loam, ruffled here by a deadfall and there by a bit of ledge. He could rest his eyes on the pool that consistently served up brown trout measured in pounds, not inches. Usually gregarious and quick with a self-depreciating quip punctuated with a quiet chuckle, Roger would sit there alone on his perch, seldom speaking.

When he raised his eyes from his beloved valley, what Roger saw was a gently rippled scape of picture-book farms with bands of corn and alfalfa ribboning the contours of the land. He knew each farm, knew each family that worked the fields and raised the fodder that filled the silos to feed the dairy cows during Wisconsin's long and often bitter winters.

They, like he, were the progeny of Norwegians and Germans drawn here in the 1850s by the land, wonderfully rich and cheap. The German farmers settled the highlands, where they thrust their spades through tangles of prairie grass and turned up clumps of earth colored as dark as the best bittersweet chocolate. Between their calloused palms they rubbed the soil and found it to be soft as cake flour.

The Norwegians, seeking water for their cattle, chose the valleys. They found springs that gushed from among ferns where steep and wooded slopes met the smooth and level valley floor. The water was sweet and among the cresses swam brook trout of such size that one would make a meal for a full-grown man. In their Lutheran churches, these men and women, so diligent in their duties, praised God for leading them to this land of bright promise.

The newcomers, like the Kickapoo tribe before them, had no idea why this corner of Wisconsin differed so much from the table-like prairies of Ohio, Indiana, and Illinois. They had no inkling that, had they arrived 450 million years earlier, their prairie schooners would have been sailing on a vast sea, as warm and shallow as the shoals around Florida's Keys where lime mud settles to the bottom today.

They were unaware, as well, of the gentle upthrust of the earth's crust that was just high enough to deflect the glacial ice sheets that grew from the north twenty millennia ago. They would have been terrified to contemplate this pastoral scene when it was an endless arctic desert across

which horrific storms of a week or more howled, filling the sky with dust that settled delicately, as if it were ebony snow.

Had they known how the glaciers bypassed their land and didn't fill their valleys with cobbles and boulders and sands called "drift" by geomorphologists and how the raging dust storms had deposited "loess," among the most nutritious of prairie soils, they would have been even more fervent in their heaven-sent thanks for arriving in the land known today as the Driftless Area.

To sow crops of grain, the farmers' iron plows ripped away the cap of prairie grasses. They needed lumber for buildings and cordwood for winter heat, and their saws and axes stripped the hillsides bare of timber. In time, torrential spring and summer rains sluiced the fine rich soil from the fields and denuded hillsides into the Kickapoo and its tributaries. The poorer the land became, the harder farmers had to work it. Families had to be fed and mortgages had to be paid. With every cloudburst, the land bled and devolved into a barren vista of deep gullies and muddy bottomlands.

For three-year-old Roger, life along the Kickapoo could not have been more idyllic. There were still trout in the river and his dad, Roger, Sr., taught him to fish. By the time Roger graduated from high school, he knew the stream and the hideouts of its trout as intimately as the rooms and furnishings of his parents' house. By then, the West Fork of the Kickapoo had become so smothered with sediment that its waters were fit only for put-and-take trout. The wild browns and brookies were only a memory.

Roger wanted better for the twenty-three miles of his beloved stream. At every opportunity he buttonholed Wisconsin Department of Fisheries Biologist Dave Vetrano about the restoration of the West Fork. He pressed for the use of trout stamp money to halt sideways erosion on curves. He wanted to rip-rap the worst bends. When Vetrano and the DNR demurred, Roger would load up a dump truck with good-sized stone from his family's quarry and deposit it where he knew it would do the most good. Permits for Roger were sometimes an afterthought.

About that time, Vetrano wrote to Dave Patrick, then president of TU's Blackhawk Chapter over in Beloit. "Those guys over in Avalanche are driving me crazy," Patrick remembers the letter's lament, "I can't do work on a put-and-take stream. What can you do to help?" With roughly 100 members, Blackhawk TU was, as many Trout Unlimited chapters are, more of a fishing club than conservation organization. The members, though, turned to, raised a couple of thousand dollars, and on one hot and laborious day, hooked up with Roger and Vetrano, and constructed and installed twelve lunker structures on the West Fork.

That was the beginning. The Blackhawk chapter now had a cause. They opened their banquet to the public and were soon raising around $10,000 per year. They equipped a trailer with a compressor and generator and an array of power saws and drills. Soon they could knock together and install 100 cribs in a day.

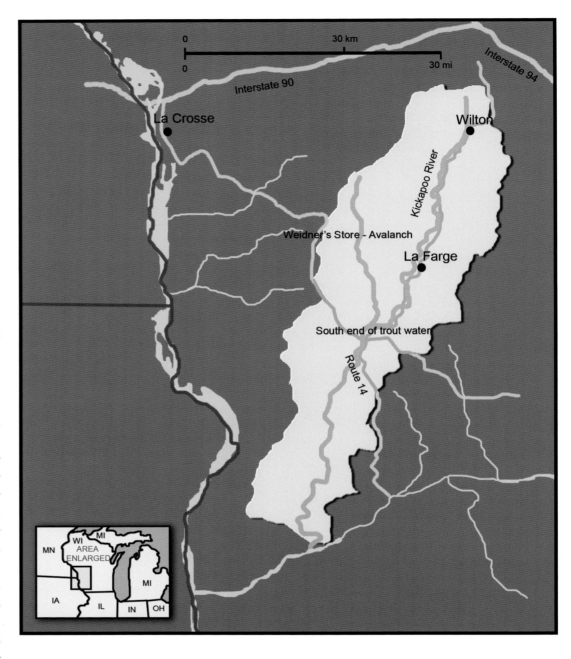

The gentle creeks of the Driftless Area were once filled with brookies. (right)

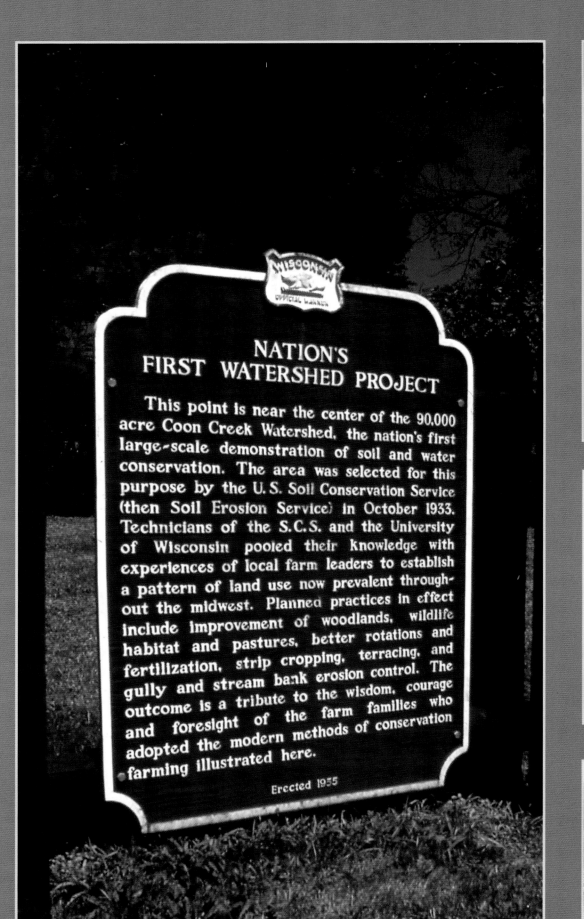

NATION'S FIRST WATERSHED PROJECT

This point is near the center of the 90,000 acre Coon Creek Watershed, the nation's first large-scale demonstration of soil and water conservation. The area was selected for this purpose by the U.S. Soil Conservation Service (then Soil Erosion Service) in October 1933. Technicians of the S.C.S. and the University of Wisconsin pooled their knowledge with experiences of local farm leaders to establish a pattern of land use now prevalent throughout the midwest. Planned practices in effect include improvement of woodlands, wildlife habitat and pastures, better rotations and fertilization, strip cropping, terracing, and gully and stream bank erosion control. The outcome is a tribute to the wisdom, courage and foresight of the farm families who adopted the modern methods of conservation farming illustrated here.

Erected 1955

That first project on the West Fork grew into the Kickapoo Watershed Conservation Project, TU's second Home Rivers Initiative. Launched in 1996, the project's goals were to expand the fishery, increase awareness and support for the watershed's protection, and provide a framework for sustainable management of the resource. At its head was Laura Hewitt, who'd just earned her masters in conservation biology and sustainable development from the University of Wisconsin-Madison. Hewitt, a disciple of long-time TU leader Steve Born, took to the Kickapoo like a brookie returning to a spring creek. Working with Roger and his friends, Hewitt embarked on a campaign to help landowners understand the economic and aesthetic as well as environmental benefits of stream restoration on their farms.

The successful collaboration in the Kickapoo watershed among TU, community groups, and state and federal agencies blossomed in 2006 into the Driftless Area Restoration Effort, a unique partnership among four states—Illinois, Iowa, Minnesota, and Wisconsin—to restore brook trout in the 24,000 square miles that constitute the westernmost reaches of this char's original range. More than $1.5 million has now been earmarked for the work in the Driftless Area.

Roger had an inkling of where all this was headed as he sat there on his knoll. And there can be no doubt that he understood the frailty of the environment. Cancer took him in the fall of 2006, when wild brookies and browns were just beginning to spawn.

How's the Fishing? The West Fork of the Kickapoo is

ear-marked for catch-and-release, artificial-lures only. Tan caddis, attractors, and terrestrials are the go-to flies. If you plan a trip to the region, spend time on Timber Coulee and Trout Run, a pair of terrific streams in the Driftless region. Pack your 4-weight, settle into a bed and breakfast, and plan to stay a while.

The only thing Roger Widner loved more than fishing was running his backhoe to improve the West Branch of the Kickapoo. (middle left)

CHAPTER 17

Little Tennessee, Tennessee

 When Hernando De Soto and his 600 conquistadores swung down the Little Tennessee River in the summer of 1540, he passed through the Cherokee towns of Tellassee and Chote. These were the first Europeans that the Cherokees, gentle farmers in the main, had ever seen. By the 1600s, English traders from Virginia and South Carolina had begun filtering through the country. Some took native wives and settled. The French, eager to cement their conquest of the Mississippi Valley, formed alliances with all of the tribes but the Cherokees, who remained friends with the British on the eve of the French and Indian War.

In 1756, the British built their first fort west of the Appalachians, where Tellico Creek joins the Little Tennessee. It was named for the Earl of Loudoun. When Captain Raymond Demere moved his 200 troops into the star-shaped log-palisaded enclosure, he said that the Cherokees "call it the Fort to put Horses, Cows, and Hogs in, but I differ in opinion with them for it would not (for that purpose) be sufficient." Conflicts between the English and the Indians occurred almost immediately, and the friendship between the allies soured. The Cherokees laid siege to Fort Loudoun in 1760, and the British were forced to surrender within two months. The Cherokees let the 240 soldiers, women, and children leave the fort safely, but then attacked them the following day, murdering 30 of the refugees.

A truce was brokered a year later, and British lieutenant Henry Timberlake volunteered to visit the Cherokees along the Little Tennessee to explain the peace and to gather intelligence. Timberlake was a skilled mapmaker and journalist. His map, "A draught of the Cherokee Country . . ." and his accompanying *Memoirs* provide an amazingly accurate

and detailed inventory of towns along the river. The legend on the map included the "Names of the Principal or Headmen of each Town and what Fighting Men, they send to War," a total of 809 in March 1762. Two of the ten village sites were flooded when Chilhowee Dam, owned by Alcoa, became operational in 1955, and the rest, including Chote, capital of the Cherokee Nation, were inundated with construction of the Tennessee Valley Authority's bitterly opposed Tellico Dam in 1979. Located a few hundred yards upstream from the Little T's confluence with the Tennessee River, this plug of concrete and steel is the sole headstone for thousands and thousands of flooded graves of the Cherokee, a culture that spanned a millennium and was the most advanced native civilization in the East.

The Cherokees knew nothing of trout. The river that flowed past their fields was warm, populated with catfish, suckers, and prehistoric gar. The TVA's construction of 480-foot-high Fontana Dam in North Carolina created a cold tailwater plume that extended more than forty miles, all the way down to Fort Loudoun. Browns and rainbows were stocked after

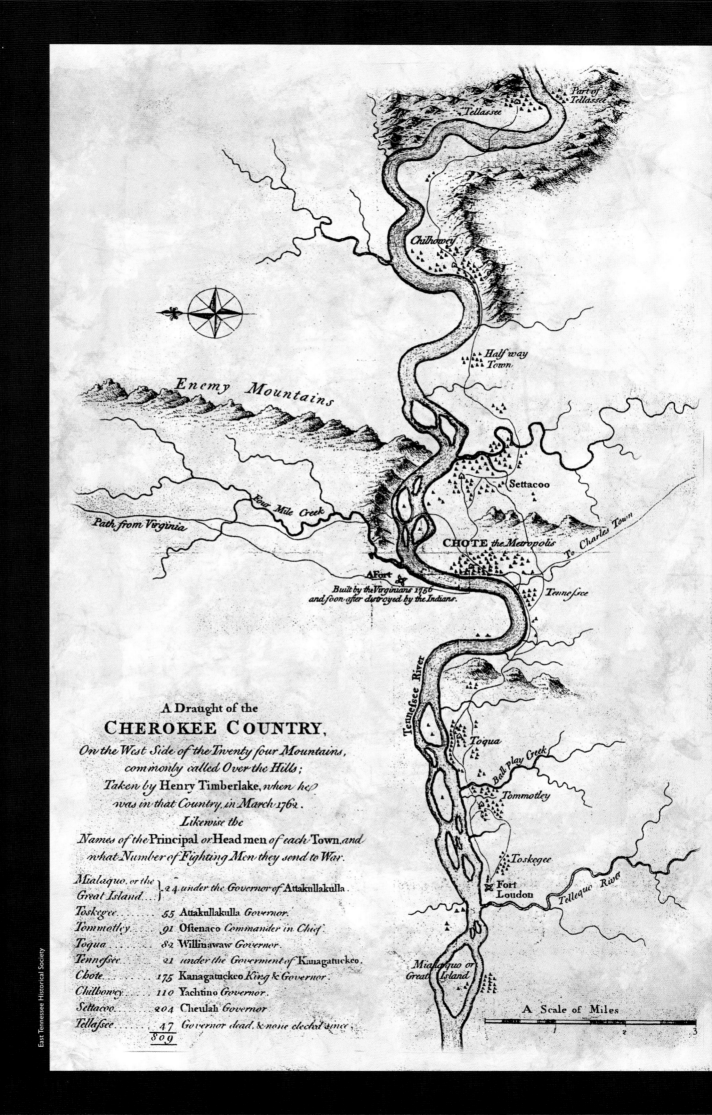

A Draught of the
CHEROKEE COUNTRY,
On the West Side of the Twenty four Mountains,
commonly called Over the Hills;
Taken by Henry Timberlake, when he
was in that Country, in March 1762.
Likewise the
Names of the Principal or Head men of each Town, and
what Number of Fighting Men they send to War.

Mialaquo, or the Great Island	24	under the Governor of Attakullakulla.
Toskegee	55	Attakullakulla Governor.
Tommotley	91	Ostenaco Commander in Chief.
Toqua	82	Willinawaw Governor.
Tennessee	21	under the Government of Kanagatuckeo.
Chote	175	Kanagatuckeo King & Governor.
Chilhowey	110	Yachtino Governor.
Settacoo	204	Cheulah Governor
Tellassee	47	Governor dead, & none elected since
	809	

the dam was sealed in 1944. By the 1950s and '60s, the Little T had become the worst-kept secret in all of troutdom. Anglers flocked to Hoss Holt's roadside shop below Chilhowee Dam, launched their jonboats when the dam was generating, and cast big plugs for big browns. When the water was off, anglers filtered down dozens of dirt lanes, hiked across the sites of Cherokee villages and picked up shards of pottery or, when luck was good, arrowheads. When the water was up, they cast nymphs designed by Eddy George—the George Harvey of the Little Tennessee—and caught big trout, and lots of them. My family had moved to Knoxville in 1957, and a decade later, when I should have been doing my homework, I fished the Little T with my brother Sam. Our favorite spot was below Howard's Bluff, where the Cherokees had built a "vee" weir of flat rocks carefully placed to span the river and funnel fish into the woven baskets of waiting Indian women.

From the moment the damming of the Little T was proposed in 1936, the project could not be justified for flood control or power generation, the TVA's *raison d'être*. Conceived as an extension of the main river Fort Loudoun Dam, less than a mile up the main river from the Little T's mouth, the project was nixed by the War Production Board in the early 1940s. By 1959, however, the TVA had pretty much run out of rivers to dam. Yet many of the TVA's senior staff traced their tenure back to the agency's creation in 1933. Damming rivers was what they knew. Thousands were employed in engineering and construction divisions. With no dam projects, they'd be thrown out of work. TVA chairman Aubrey "Red" Wagner saw no reason for TVA to change its spots. Dams meant jobs. Bright new industrial cities would rise from lakeshores, especially in the valley of the Little T where major railroads and highways crossed. New cities would bring prosperity where farms were poor, incomes were marginal, and young people were fleeing for jobs in the cities. Or so TVA management and politicians believed. Both were hooked on the "model cities" movement sweeping the country in the early 1970s.

The Boeing Corporation, which was to be the developer of the new city on the Little T, was also hooked. It was to be called Timberlake, after Lieutenant Henry. But for Timberlake to become a reality, the TVA needed to land a big industrial fish and secure millions in federal funding. Neither materialized, and Boeing backed out. Its model city nothing more than colored drawings, TVA continued to insist that Tellico would be an economic boon to the region. Yet, as they had since the 1940s, neither the TVA's or any other economists could find numbers to support the agency's assertion. Undaunted by facts, Wagner forged ahead. Construction began in 1967.

Resistance from the environmental community was stiffening. In 1970, the conservation-minded Environmental Defense Fund, joined by Trout Unlimited and Tom Moser, whose farm had been condemned, filed suit to halt Tellico, charging that the TVA had not filed a complete environmental impact statement. They won their claim in 1971, and construction of the dam was halted. It started up again in early 1973, after the TVA filed its EIS.

About that same time, Hank Hill had been asked to take a breather from the rigors of the University of Tennessee's law school because his grades weren't so good. Assuaging his unhappy state of affairs over brews with a bunch of biology students, Hill learned that one of their professors, David Etnier, had discovered a tiny species of perch—the snail darter—that appeared to exist nowhere else except at the mouth of the Little T. Etnier, as it turns out, was a staunch opponent of the dam, and was ecstatic about his discovery. Hill was no fan of the dam either. With the assistance of one of his law professors, Zyg Plater, and local attorneys Joe Congleton and Boone Dougherty, Hill petitioned to have the snail darter listed as endangered under the newly passed Endangered Species Act. With the aid of scores of TUers from Tennessee and Georgia who flew

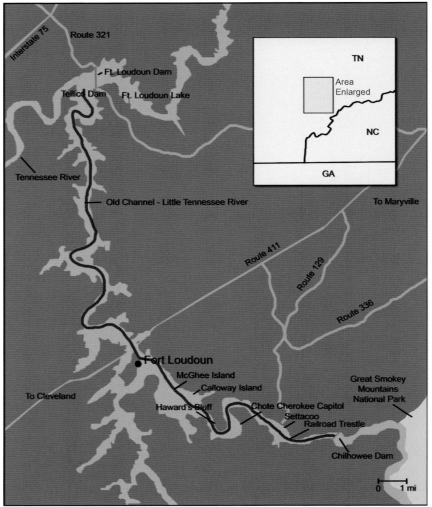

Anglers work a riffle on the Little T before it was dammed. (above)

Flooding the valley forced scores of families from their farms and submerged forever sacred towns of the Cherokee Nation. (upper right)

TU in Action

TU's victory before the U.S. Supreme Court validated the power of the Endangered Species Act to halt construction of a dam.

The Tellico Dam case helped establish that the economic value of recreation must be accorded equal weight with commerce and industry.

Though Congress exempted the Tellico Dam from regulation by the EPA, the hard-fought campaign convinced the TVA to build weirs that support trout fisheries below Norris, South Holston, and Cherokee dams.

into Washington to make the case, Hill and his group were successful. The snail darter was determined to be endangered, and the Environmental Protection Agency (EPA) ordered that work be stopped on Tellico Dam.

To make a very long story short, the TVA sought to overturn the EPA's ruling in federal court. The court ruled that the dam would destroy the endangered darter, but failed to enjoin TVA from continuing work. Hill, TU, and other dam opponents appealed the decision and won in Sixth District court, the verdict of which was affirmed by the U.S. Supreme Court. The high court issued a permanent injunction against further construction in 1978.

Matt Braughler

It was a stunning victory for TU, the Cherokees, the environmental community, and endangered species everywhere. Justice had spoken, but Congress had not. Tennessee Senator Howard Baker pushed through legislation that amended the Endangered Species Act to provide exemptions for federal projects where the economic benefit might outweigh the value of the species. A board of experts, immediately dubbed the "God Squad," was impaneled. To Baker's acute disappointment, they also found no economic merit in the Tellico project.

Baker was not finished, however. He was well aware that since the earliest white settlement of the Tennessee valley, horses had been traded in its pastures and barrels of pork had been shipped downriver. The flesh had changed but the notion had not. President Jimmy Carter, who was eager to secure ratification of the Panama Canal Treaty, needed Baker's vote. The horse was traded. The Carter administration did not stand in the way of Baker's amendment to fund the Tellico Dam. The river's fate was sealed; the dam gates were closed in 1979.

New leadership had taken reins of the TVA while the Tellico controversy was playing out in court and Congress. S. David Freeman had replaced Wagner as chairman. Freeman told Congleton that the TVA was beginning to understand the economic benefits of tailwater fisheries, and committed $200 million to mitigate downstream dead zones created by oxygen-depleted water released by its dams. As a result, oxygenating aeration weirs have been built below Norris, South Holston, and Cherokee dams and minimum flows have been established. The South Holston and neighboring Watauga River have become, arguably, the best tailwater fisheries in the Southeast, magnets for traveling anglers, and an economic boon to the tri-cities of Bristol, Johnson City, and Kingsport in northeast Tennessee and southwest Virginia.

How's the Fishing? Though Tellico Lake is stocked with trout, it's not much of a trout fishery. From their bass boats, anglers cast plugs to the shoreline or around flooded silos in pursuit of smallmouth and largemouth bass instead. Much better trout fishing bets are the Hiwassee, about 50 miles south near Cleveland; the Clinch, 40 miles north; or the South Holston, 125 miles up Interstate 81 near Bristol. The Hiwassee is streamer water; the Clinch is known for its midge hatches; and the South Holston, the best of the trio, hatches clouds of mayflies and provides the best angler access.

CHAPTER 18

Muddy Creek, North Carolina

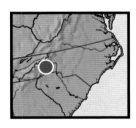

As far as farms around Dysartsville, North Carolina, go, Wayne Landis's 115-acre place on the south fork of Hopper's Creek isn't overly large. His eight brothers and sisters, including ninety-four-year-old Georgia, were all born there; so were his mother and his grandfather, Joseph Benjamin Landis, who was a lieutenant in the local company of North Carolina's Civil War militia.

Twenty years after the war, the farm was up, running, and more prosperous than it had ever been. Wayne's grandfather built a big white frame farmhouse around this time. His father, Joseph B. Landis II, added on to it the year before Wayne was born. That was 1930. Georgia remembers crops of cotton, peanuts, rye, corn, sorghum, and tobacco. There was also an orchard, a big vegetable garden, and cattle, sheep, and hogs behind the fence.

The land was productive enough, but marshy patches lined the stream that meandered through the fields. The wetlands couldn't be plow or planted and calves sometimes became mired in the mud. In the 1920s, Joseph B. II decided to take care of that problem by cutting a straight channel down the center of the stream. He dug ditches and installed tiles, some of fired clay and others of log, to divert rain and groundwater directly into the channel. Then he covered the tiles over with dirt deep enough to plow. When he was finished, he'd added a dozen tillable acres to his farm. He wasn't the only farmer who ditched and tiled his fields, either, as most of his neighbors did, as did their neighbors and the neigh-

bors beyond. The practice was actively promoted by early soil conservation theory, a kind of oxymoron when you think about the name in light of modern environmental understanding.

As it turns out, the soil under these low foothills of the Piedmont contains a good deal of clay and sand. Heavy rains—and this area sees more than its share of hurricane remnants—cause the soil to erode rapidly. Mud thick as thin concrete sluiced down the channelized branches, heading to the nearest biggest stream, the creek that drained the watershed. In this case the slurry flowed into the aptly named Muddy Creek. Muddy Creek, in turn, annually poured 30,000 tons of ugly orange sediment into the Catawba River tailwater one mile downstream from Bridgewater Dam, which impounds Lake James. The seventeen miles of river, from the dam down through Morganton, is the big river trout fishery closest to the largest number of North Carolinians.

Squeak Smith, an Air Force F-4 Phantom backseater before settling in the foothills west of Morganton in late 1986, had his eye on the Catawba tailwater. So did the Table Rock Chapter of Trout Unlimited. Every

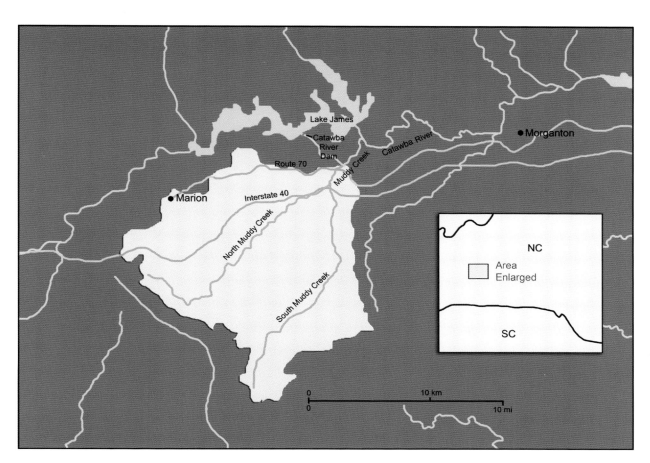

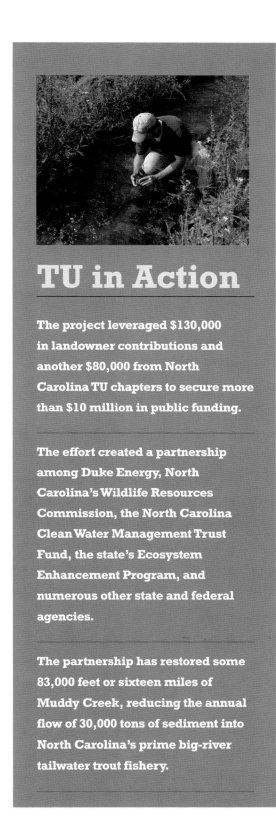

TU in Action

The project leveraged $130,000 in landowner contributions and another $80,000 from North Carolina TU chapters to secure more than $10 million in public funding.

The effort created a partnership among Duke Energy, North Carolina's Wildlife Resources Commission, the North Carolina Clean Water Management Trust Fund, the state's Ecosystem Enhancement Program, and numerous other state and federal agencies.

The partnership has restored some 83,000 feet or sixteen miles of Muddy Creek, reducing the annual flow of 30,000 tons of sediment into North Carolina's prime big-river tailwater trout fishery.

Muddy Creek has never seen a trout. Reclamation of hog farms and mitigation of other historic agriculture in the creek's watershed ensures the future for trout in the Catawba River. (left)

time a cloud burst over Muddy Creek, the spate pumped hundreds of gallons of clayish muck into the river, suffocating the spawning redds of brown trout and natal zones for caddis and mayflies. Yet Duke Energy, which generates electricity at Bridgewater Dam, and North Carolina's Wildlife Resources Commission (NCWRC) had long believed that the Catawba could become a trophy trout fishery. The challenge was daunting. The 110-square-mile Muddy Creek watershed and more than 340 miles of forks, branches, and tributaries that flowed through farms such as the Landis place needed to be cleaned up.

In 1998, Smith, then serving on TU's National Resource Board, found his target and the Muddy Creek project took off. He corralled those with vested interests in the watershed: Duke Energy, NCWRC, the Foothills Conservancy, the U.S. Fish and Wildlife Foundation, the governments of Burke and McDowell counties and the City of Morganton, the National Resource Conservation Service, and North Carolina's TU Council. Based on studies done by Duke Energy and NCWRC, the partners outlined four priorities: restore natural channels, reestablish riparian forest, exclude livestock, and protect intact headwaters and bottom lands.

Nothing could happen without the voluntary consent of landowners, and for them, the times were changing. Few farms supported the families that lived on the land, and they hadn't for a long time. Since he turned twenty, Wayne Landis had been augmenting his farm income with a full-time job, in his case with the Soil Conservation Service. Working on survey and fencing crews, he helped build nine earthen flood-control dams in the Muddy Creek watershed. And once the dams were built, he mowed the grass and patched washouts when the soil of the dams gave way. He saw those lakes stocked with bluegills and bass that grew "long as your leg." He never fished for them, preferring instead the sweet meat of crappies.

Landis continued to grow sorghum on the family farm, which he sold to grandnephew Steve Melton in 2007. One sultry August some time ago Landis made 2,464 gallons of syrup in six days. That was his best month ever. But he's seventy-seven now, and has quit making molasses. Today he grows enough field peas, okra, and tomatoes for himself, still runs a few head of cattle, and raises a handful of hogs. He's acquired quite a local reputation for his sausage. His secret: "Mostly it's being fresh," he says. "I don't let the meat lay around." He grinds the pork the same day the hog's skinned and butchered, a chore that's never undertaken when the weather is hot. If you press him, he might tell you that he uses more spices than most folks. He's well aware that his sausage-making days are numbered.

In some ways, Landis's nephew typifies the new wave of farmers moving into the Muddy Creek watershed. He plans to refurbish the farmhouse, preferring its wide front porch and high ceilinged rooms to factory- or stick-built modern homes. Melton grows organic blueberries and raises some cattle. Like his great uncle, he works in the field of soil conservation, but there the resemblance ends.

Soil conservation in Wayne's day was based on two conflicting concepts. Meanders were straightened, ditches were dug, and tiles were laid to drain the land as fast as possible. Dams were built to slow down runoff, prevent floods, and contain sediment. With a degree in environmental health with an emphasis on aquatic ecology, Melton is a adherent to Dave Rosgen's principles of stream classification, geomorphology, and rehabilitation. A field biologist with Equinox Environmental, Melton relies on the restoration of natural meander channels with wetlands and flood plains to absorb energy, nutrients, and moisture when streams are flooded. Using Rosgen's concepts, he has coordinated most of the thirty restoration projects that have taken place on Muddy Creek. As this was being written, he was scheduled to oversee stream restoration on the Landis place next.

Fishing drew angler-conservationist Squeak Smith (inset) to the mountains of western North Carolina. He's forged the partnerships that are removing the mud from Muddy Creek and nurturing big browns in the Catawba.

How's the Fishing?

With gentle riffles and long, cold runs, the seventeen-mile tailwater running from below Bridgewater Dam through Morganton holds the potential of becoming North Carolina's premier big trout river. That's big in both cases. The river is similar in size and promise to the West Branch of the Delaware River in New York. North Carolina stocks it annually with 50,000 fingerling half-wild browns. Trout of up to twenty-four inches have been taken. Time your trip for May. Hatches are most prolific then. The best tactic is to float to a shoal and then wade.

Matt Braughler

**Without the voluntary consent of landowners,
rivers like the Catawba wouldn't stand a chance.**

CHAPTER 19

Nushagak River, Alaska

Scraggly beeches with silver, peeling bark and whitish-green leaves vie with stands of spruce for space on the height of land rimming the west bank of the Nushagak River. For as long as anyone can remember, the village of Ekwok has occupied the high ground here, eighty miles upriver from Dillingham. In Yup'ik, the language of the local native Alaskans (also called Yup'ik), Ekwok means "end of the bluff." A big blue school sits on the upper terrace above the river, near the Ekwok Bible Chapel with its plain belfry. In the adjacent cemetery, framed with a white picket fence, each grave is marked with a five-foot-tall Russian Orthodox cross and decorated with bright red, yellow, and blue plastic flowers.

Nobody remembers how many generations of Yup'iks have occupied the village. It is the oldest on the Nushagak, the largest tributary to Bristol Bay. The Yup'ik settled here because of the prolific runs of Pacific salmon, the profusion of ripe salmon berries and blue berries in late July

"We take our grandchildren to gather berries and wild spinach and celery. They learn responsibility that way. They learn to respect the land. In return, the land and the river will take care of them." —Luki Akelkok, Yup'ik elder

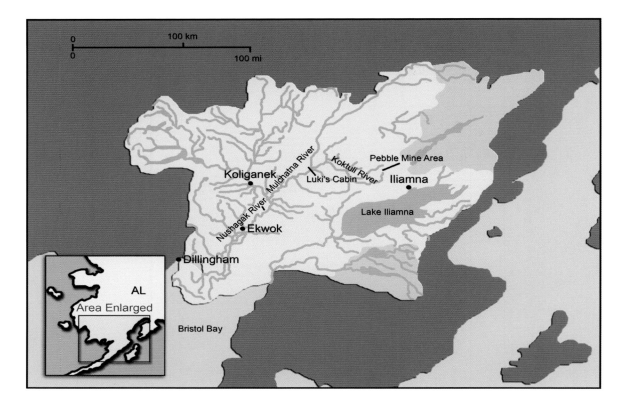

and August, and the proximity to large numbers of moose that inhabit the boggy tundra and caribou that use the centuries-old migration routes that criss-cross the region. The hunter-gatherer
culture more than sustains Ekwok. It is one of the reasons, but not the only one, that the village's
population has grown from 70 in 1980 to 138 today.

Most of the land surrounding Ekwok—some 1,000 square miles, roughly the size Rhode Island, including all the waters that flow into Bristol Bay—are slated for hard rock mineral extrac-
tion. At the core of what may become the largest single mining district in the United States is the
Pebble Mine, sixty miles as the eagle flies to the east-northeast in the hills above Lake Iliamna.
Though Pebble Mine officials boast of creating the largest gold and copper mine in the world,
they promise "no net loss" of habitat. Yup'ik leaders see the Pebble Mine as Pandora's box.

No one is more eloquent in opposing the mine than seventy-one-year-old Luki Akelkok, a
Yup'ik whose roots in Ekwok are as deep as the glacial soil. Forced from school when he was ten
by the death of his father, as the oldest son it was his duty to fish and hunt and pick the berries to
provide food for his mother, brothers, sisters, and grandparents in whose house he was raised.
Then, just as now, there was no store in Ekwok. All food had to be gathered and preserved.
Though flour, sugar, milk, and shortening were delivered by boat and later, by air, they were then,
as they are now, frightfully expensive.

Salmon was and is the mainstay. Gill-netted, it is cleaned and sent downriver to canneries in
Dillingham. More and more is now also iced and flown out fresh to cities across North America.
Every household in the village also has a shed where filets are hung to dry in the wind. In earlier
days, much was salted, to be reconstituted later in the manner favored by New Englanders with
their cod. Some portions are considered delicacies. The humps of red salmon, for example, are
cut from the backs of the fish, soaked in salted water, and eaten raw.

Brian Kraft, owner of the Alaska Sportsman's Lodge, on the outflow from Lake Iliamna, and
one of the founders of the Bristol Bay Alliance, had arranged for me to hook up with Luki. (The
Bristol Bay Alliance's motto? "Pure water is more precious than gold.") So I may see the Nushagak
and learn more about its salmon, Luki takes me by flat-bottomed skiff 120 miles up to its confluence with the Mulchatna, then on to the Swan, where it's joined by the Koktuli. Luki has a cabin
here. To the north are the Jack Rabbit Hills. To the east, across a low range of unnamed mountains, lies the site of Pebble Mine, on the headwaters of the Koktuli. Flotillas of sockeye salmon,
brilliant red after spawning, chase each other in the shallow run of the river in front of his cabin.

Mine officials plan two earth dams, one 4.3 miles long and 740 feet high, to hold back toxic tailings in one of the world's most active earthquake zones.

*TU, coalitions of native people, commercial fisheries, and
sportsmen are all allied against Pebble Mine. (right)*

Protect clean water and wild Alaska salmon
PEBBLE
http://renewableresourcescoalition.org
Paid for by Renewable Resources Coalition • 500 L Street, Suite 502, Anchorage, AK 99501

"For them, it is all about money. For us, it is about our grandchildren and their children's children. The mines will close one day, maybe not for fifty or sixty years. What will happen then?"

If the earth tailing dams fail, millions of tons of slurry will poison major watersheds where Bristol Bay's famed salmon spawn. (left)

Bear tracks the size of dinner plates trace the edge of the sandbar where I walk. I'm armed only with a 6-weight.

"What will happen to the salmon, John?" he asks me as we sit on folding chairs on his porch. "They [mine officials] say there will be no net loss. What does that mean? They plan to pump a lake dry and to build a dam 4.3 miles long and 740 feet high for tailings. How can there be no loss? And what if the dam fails?" he asks.

This is no idle question. The Denali fault passes close to the proposed mine. As recently as November 2002, an earthquake measuring 7.9 caused twenty-nine feet of horizontal offset. The Good Friday quake of 1964 devastated Anchorage and many towns along and inland from the Gulf of Alaska. It charted 9.2 on the Richter scale. On average, Alaska experiences one quake measuring 7 or more every year.

An earthquake could easily rupture the proposed earthen tailings dam and flush billions of gallons of sediment slurry down the Koktuli and ultimately into Bristol Bay. A huge tailing lake is also planned for Upper Talarik Creek, one of Alsaka's premier rainbow fisheries. Should a quake cause that dam to fail, it doesn't take much to imagine the plume of sediment sludge would flood into Lake Iliamna, home of North America's only population of freshwater seals.

If Pebble is established, that's just the first step, Luki says, staring up his beloved Koktuli over thousands of acres the state plans to open to mining. "Salmon are in every stream. If mining comes, where will they spawn? Without salmon, what will we eat? The noise from helicopters has already scared away the caribou."

Salmon and trout are the species most visibly endangered by mining, yet the threat is much deeper. "I will not live to see what the mine does," he states. "But what does it mean for my grandchildren? Mine officials promise 1,000 new jobs. What jobs will there be for us? They want mining experience, and we do not have that. Most good jobs will go to outsiders.

"We take our grandchildren hunting and fishing. As families, we take them to gather berries and wild spinach and celery. They learn responsibility that way. They learn to respect the land. In return, the land and the river will take care of them."

Later, after we have boated back downriver, and finished a dinner of baked fresh salmon prepared by Pauline, Luki's wife, we go to sit in his sweat lodge. The temperature reaches 200°F, something I am not used to.

"It is the same story, John," he says rubbing a cloth dipped in cooling water over his closely cropped grey hair. "They think we are dumb and cannot see. But they are the ones who don't see. For them, it is all about money. For us, it is about our grandchildren and their children's children. The mines will close one day, maybe not for fifty or sixty years. What will happen then? What will happen if the salmon are all gone?"

Brandon Cole

How's the Fishing? The river is famed for huge runs of king salmon in June and July, sockeyes in July, and cohos from July until September. The Nushagak's many tributaries hold rainbows that fatten up on salmon eggs and flesh and sometimes reach weights of ten pounds. Numerous outfitters, like Luki, operate lodges and provide guides. Use light saltwater fly tackle for kings, and stiffish 7-weights for the others. Pack bright streamers, egg and leach patterns, and bombers. Who knows? You might entice a salmon to the surface.

Ted V. Wood

South Fork Snake River, Idaho

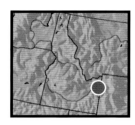

The fish hit one of Harry Murray's No. 6 black stremphs deep in a seam between arguing currents, just where it should. The instant it came on the line, I could tell it was a heavy fish. It did not run or jump. Rather it threw dogged body punches, standing toe to toe, bobbing and weaving, duking it out at close range. Ten minutes later, I had it close to the surface. At first, guide Shaun Lawson and I thought it was a big cutthroat, but then it rolled and the flash of vermillion told us the truth. Rainbow. I backed it into Shaun's waiting net. He swung it into the boat. The fish went in a good twenty inches. I reached down into the net, grasped the fly, and flipped it from its jaw. Done, I straightened, looked at Shaun with a grin, and said, "That was fun. What's next?"

"Better kill it," Shaun said. Had this been any other Idaho river besides the South Fork of the Snake, we'd have released this lovely wild trout. Instead, I opened my penknife and plunged its fine blade into the base of the rainbow's brain. In a twitch it was dead. This fish was the first trout I'd intentionally killed in a dozen years, and it was not comfortable for me or for Shaun. Whelped by Mike, his dad, on Henry's Fork, he has catch-and-release in his genes. Shaun is carrying on the family tradition, working to rehabilitate the South Fork, just as his father has worked for Henry's.

This was the spring of 2004, the first such season the South Fork had been open for fishing in a long, long time. The order of the day was catch and kill rainbows, one leg of a three-pronged plan to restore Yellowstone cutthroats to the South Fork of the Snake from Twin Falls,

about 240 miles upstream, to Palisades Dam. In addition, flows on the river are being managed to maximize cutthroat spawning success and minimize that of rainbows. Aggressive plans to remove rainbows and return cutthroats to their native spawning grounds have also been put in place on Rainey, Pine, Palisades, and Burns creeks.

The plans were developed by Jim Fredericks, Idaho Department of Fish and Game; TU's Idaho staff, headed by Scott Yates; the Bureau of Land Management; the U.S. Forest Service; the U.S. Fish and Wildlife Service; and a potpourri of others. Funding has come from a number of partners, including Mark Rockefeller, the National Fish and Wildlife Foundation, the Jackson Hole One Fly Foundation, the U.S. Forest Service, the Idaho Department of Fish and Game, the Idaho Fish and

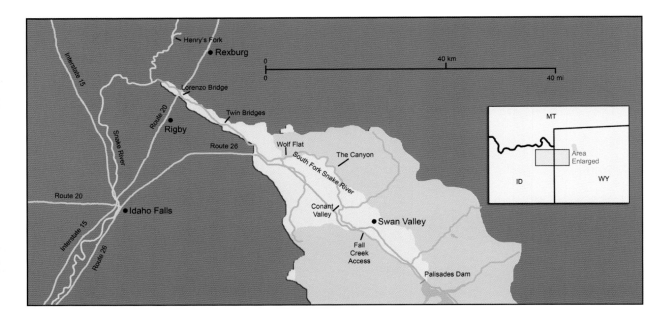

Wildlife Foundation, the U.S. Bureau of Land Management, Snake River Cutthroats, and Idaho Panhandle TU chapters.

According to Shaun, who is the manager of South Fork Outfitters, which operates in conjunction with South Fork Lodge just upstream of the Conant boat access, the plan seems to be working. Cutthroat catches (all are released) have increased both in quantity and size, with twelve- to fourteen-inch trout common and more and more twenty-inchers being taken every season. Creel surveys show that anglers are catching and killing more rainbows, due in large part to the opening of the river to year-round fishing in 2004.

Most of us make our jaunts to the South Fork in September or October, when nights are frosty, elk are moving down from the mountains, and grouse hunting and fly fishing go hand in hand. But you owe it to yourself to fish these waters in late April or May, when skwala stoneflies, those gargantuan floating bundles of protein, draw vicious strikes from cutts, rainbows, and browns. The river looks different then, too. The muted grays and tans and yellows from withered grasses, dried sage, and the fluttering fall leaves of cottonwoods are replaced by the soft green of new grass, the frosty purple of sage just leafed out, and the brilliant chromium of arrowhead balsam root blasting forth on south-facing slopes. Yellow-headed blackbirds and male western tanagers cavort in the newly verdant willows. Bald eagles and white pelicans ride the thermals, and sandhill cranes strut the riverside marshes, staking out nesting sites. The Snake River Valley is utterly delightful at this time of year.

We fish the river for two days, floating the section from Fall Creek to Conant on the first day and then from Conant to Fisher Bottom, below Antelope Flat, on the next. The evening after our last float, the lodge's chef, Dan Davis, retrieved my rainbow from the refrigerator, toasted a quarter cup of almonds beneath his broiler, melted four ounces of butter in a sauté pan, added two tablespoons each of Worcestershire sauce and fresh lemon juice, reduced it by one third, lowered the heat, added the almonds, and let it rest. He removed head and tail from the trout, butterflied it and removed the bones, dabbed a little sauce on it, and laid it skin down under the broiler so the flesh was lightly seared but no more. Lowering the rack, he gave the filet three minutes more, then slipped it on a warm platter, drizzled the remaining lemon almond sauce over it, garnished it with cubes of fresh yellow and green squash, roasted red peppers, and little browned potatoes, and slid it before our noses. I don't remember the white wine. Who would?

I was awakened in the morning by the *thawka . . . wak, thawka . . . wak* of a chopper lazing over Conant access. Pulling on my duds, I stepped out onto the porch of my cabin and saw a cluster of

TU in Action

In 2002, TU and the Snake River Cutthroats, a joint Federation of Fly Fishers/TU chapter, established a Home Rivers Initiative on the South Fork. To date, cutthroat spawning habitat has been restored on three tributaries—Pritchard, Garden, and Rainey creeks—and work continues on two others (Pine and Burns).

A 2003 TU-funded economic impact study found that fishing and boating on the Upper Snake River has created 1,460 jobs and $46 million dollars in income.

TU is working with the Bureau of Reclamation to sustain minimum flows below the Palisades Dam and to adjust spring flows to favor cutthroat reproduction.

Harvesting South Fork rainbows is resulting in larger catches of bigger cutthroats.

You owe it to yourself to fish the South Fork in May. Wildflowers, carpet slopes, and morel mushrooms pop forth in grasses beneath frothy green cottonwoods.

red lights flashing at the launch ramp. "Oh, no!" I thought, "there must have been an accident." I grabbed my cameras and notebook and raced over to Shaun's fly shop. A few cars were parked in front. As I burst through the front door, something seemed odd. There were no patrons gathered at the window, no hushed conversations. One women and a clerk were picking out streamers, Shaun was showing somebody a rod, and another customer was over by the shirts. Everything actually seemed quite normal.

"Hey," I said loudly, to alert them to the disaster. "Hey, was there an accident? What's all the commotion at the launch ramp? It doesn't look good."

"What accident?" the guy behind the counter asked in an offhandish manner.

"The flashing lights, the helicopters, the police cars, the ambulance . . ."

He grinned at me as you would at someone who was slightly addled. "Oh, that's just Dick. The vice president likes to fish here."

Tim Romano

How's the Fishing? Make tracks for the South Fork in late April and early May. The river is warm enough then for trout to feed on the surface, and you'll encounter few other anglers. Morel mushrooms grow to eight inches high and nicely complement the thick rainbows you'll harvest in the name of conservation.

CHAPTER 21

South Platte, Colorado

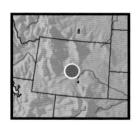

There are those, and I'm one of them, to whom a thin arch dam is a thing of beauty. I come by it naturally, I suppose. It's a gift or an affliction, depending on your perspective of my childhood in Knoxville, Tennessee. A favorite Sunday afternoon drive took us up U.S. 129 along the Little Tennessee River. We'd pass Chilhowee Dam, low and squat and unlovely except for gargantuan brown trout that prowled its tailwater. Then came my favorites, Calderwood and Cheoa, old, narrow, thin arch dams that bowed upstream into their lakes. They reminded me of dams in the Alps I'd seen in *National Geographic*. Later I'd learn that these dams, like the Hoover Dam, utilize the force of the lake's water to press them more tightly against the abutting rock of the gorges they plug.

It is the plugging of gorges that bothers me now. And bothered is far too mild a word—enraged is better—to describe how Colorado's trout fishing community viewed the Denver Water Board's

Mark Lance

Mark Lance

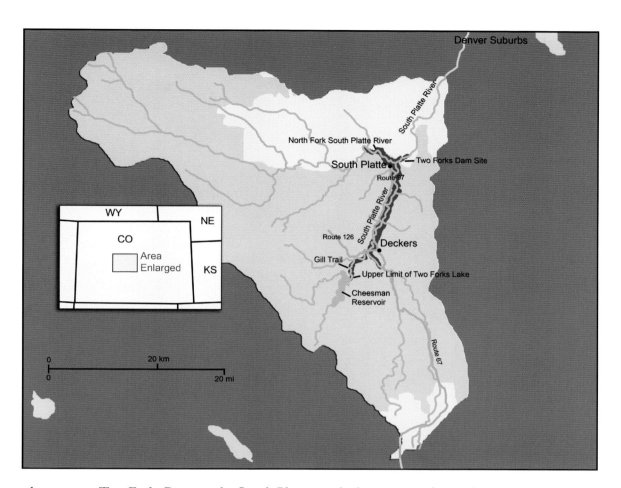

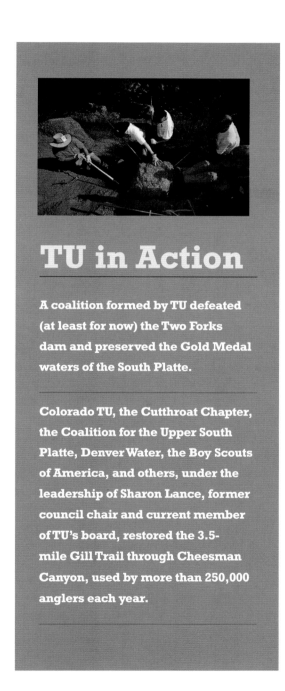

TU in Action

A coalition formed by TU defeated (at least for now) the Two Forks dam and preserved the Gold Medal waters of the South Platte.

Colorado TU, the Cutthroat Chapter, the Coalition for the Upper South Platte, Denver Water, the Boy Scouts of America, and others, under the leadership of Sharon Lance, former council chair and current member of TU's board, restored the 3.5-mile Gill Trail through Cheesman Canyon, used by more than 250,000 anglers each year.

Mastering the nymph is the key to catching fine-spotted cutts, unless of course you know your dries. (left)

plan to erect Two Forks Dam on the South Platte a mile downstream from where the river's north fork comes in. Oh, the dam itself might have been gorgeous, but its environmental impact would have been anything but. Rising 615 feet from the riverbed and with crest running nearly a third of a mile from bank to bank, Two Forks was designed with but one real purpose: augment Denver's water supply to accelerate real estate growth.

Denver Water has had its hands on the South Platte since 1905, when it constructed Cheesman Dam. It bought the small Antero Dam and Reservoir and built Elevenmile Dam on the South Platte's headwaters in 1935. The site at Two Forks seemed a natural for another dam. The long sinuous South Platte valley could hold more than 1,100,000 acre feet of water. Only twenty-four miles from Denver, it seemed the perfect place to store water diverted from the Colorado on the west slope of the Rockies. Denver Water commissioned a number of feasibility studies for Two Forks. Each came to essentially the same conclusion. The economic benefits were far outweighed by environmental liabilities. Undeterred, the board pressed on. In the mid-1980s the Colorado Council of Trout Unlimited pulled on its waders and entered the fray. Dave Taylor, then associate director for the council, led the charge.

Two Forks would have backed up the South Platte for twenty miles, to within 5,000 feet of Cheesman Dam. The dam would have flooded, among other things, the thirteen-mile Gold Medal stretch of the river. Gold Medal status is only awarded to Colorado's best trout water. At the time, in those pre-whirling-disease days, the stretch was the most productive of all of Colorado's rainbow rivers, with an estimated 744 pounds of trout per acre in Cheesman Canyon. Below Deckers, the weight per acre was halved but it was still 50 percent better than the Gunnison at Black Canyon and twice as good as the Colorado River at Parshall, or the Blue north of Silverthorne.

Taylor organized a "Save the River" press conference along the South Platte in June 1986. Curt Gowdy, a TU trustee and dean of *The American Sportsman*, the ABC television series that took guys like me hunting and fishing in places we could never afford, stated the case succinctly: "Only God can create a beautiful river and resource like this. No amount of money can replace this. Once you dam this, forget it—it's gone forever."

Prime wildlife habitat would also have been gone forever. The Two Forks reservoir would flood the grounds where elk calved and bighorn sheep, Colorado's state animal, birthed their lambs. Mule deer and Merriam's turkeys abounded in the 10,000 acres that would have been lost. It was also home to bald eagles, peregrine falcons, and other raptors, including the golden eagle; red-tailed, Cooper's, and Swainson's hawks; American kestrel; great horned owl; osprey; and prairie falcon. Perhaps most troubling was the fact that this was the last valley where a tiny dusky yellow butterfly, the Pawnee montane skipper, still survived.

The Pawnee montane skipper (*Hesperia leonardus montana*) was found only in the valley of the South Platte and its North Fork, an area covering about thirty-eight square miles. Lepidopterists, those entomologists who study butterflies and moths, believe that this small skipper is a relic from the last ice age. Its range is limited to the rare intersection of two plant communities, that of ponderosa pines with blue gama grasses and the purple flowering gayfeather, from which the butterfly sips its nourishing nectar. While Denver Water's plan would have reduced the skipper's range by 43 percent, most of its remaining range would have been located in the upper end of the North Fork. Should forest fire, accidental spraying of pesticides, or aggressive development occur, the butterfly would be threatened. No longer would children such as those of William W. G. Smith of Buffalo Creek, who captured one of the earliest known specimens in the 1880s, be able to sweep them into their butterfly nets.

The butterfly threw a final damper on Denver Water's party. It was their snail darter, that little minnow that came so close to saving the Little Tennessee River and the historic Cherokee towns along its banks. Pursuant to section 404(c) of the Clean Water Act, the Environmental Protection Agency (EPA) issued a recommended determination—the agency's opinion—to prohibit construction of Two Forks Dam and Reservoir in March 1990. It was a monumental victory for Trout Unlimited and its coalition of partners, including the Colorado Wildlife Federation, the Sierra Club, the Environmental Defense Fund, the Colorado Mountain Club, the Colorado Environmental Coalition, and the Audubon Society. And it would never have happened if William K. Reilly, newly appointed by President George H. W. Bush to head the EPA, hadn't overturned his regional supervisor, stating that Denver should pursue alternatives to Two Forks that would not cause "irreparable loss" of an "environmental treasure of national significance."

Reading the tea leaves, Denver Water sat down with Trout Unlimited and the coalition of environmental groups and over the next decade developed the South Platte Protection Plan, which was formally adopted in 2004. The plan is something of a handshake agreement. Its first priority is protecting the river in its canyons. Under the plan, the board relinquishes its rights to build the Two Forks project for twenty years and pledges no further developments of the Cheesman and Elevenmile water facilities. The plan sets flow levels beneficial to fisheries as well as floaters, and creates a stakeholder group, the South Platte Enhancement Board, to oversee the river's future. The South Platte Protection Plan's authors, among them Colorado TU executive director David Nickum, see it as giving the river a breather. It provides time to explore alternatives to quenching the thirst of Denver and its booming suburbs, but little more than that. As long as the population expands, developers will always have their eyes on the river.

How's the Fishing?

Regulations change with some frequency on the South Platte, so check them when you buy your license. Most accessible is the stretch from Deckers through Cheesman Canyon, and it's also the most finicky. The first day I fished with the redoubtable Ms. Lance, I picked up a couple of fish near Iron Springs on the Gill trail and thought, "Hey, writer, you're hot stuff." The next day we worked a lower, more technical section a quarter of a mile above Deckers. Sharon knew to fish tiny nymphs. She skunked me eight fish to nothing, smiled sweetly, and opened my beer when we got back to the car.

Russ Schnitzer

Formerly as deeply green as old bottle glass, pools in the South Platte are filling with sediment washed from steep hillsides denuded by the 138,000 acre Hayman forest fire in 2002.

History of Trout Unlimited

We've all been there. You know, when somebody says to somebody else, "You know, what we oughta do is . . ." Well, that's the way it happened. Two fishermen, both named George, were waiting to launch their boats at Burton's Landing on Michigan's Au Sable one summer morning in 1950. The first George (Mason, who was chairman of American Motors) sidled up to the second George (Griffith, newly appointed to the Michigan Conservation Commission) and said, "As you know, George, I have been national treasurer of Ducks Unlimited since it was organized. But my first love is trout fishing. I've been thinking about forming a similar organization: Trout Unlimited." Mason told Griffith to keep the following Friday night open.

That evening the two Georges convened at Mason's house on the South Branch of the Au Sable. Four others joined them: Al Hazzard, Opie Titus, Jim McKenna, and Don McLouth. Mason sought to form a group of 120 prominent anglers who'd wine and dine the state's fisheries biologists and tell them how to make trout fishing better. McLouth agreed strongly with this mission even as he worried that "someday trout fishing is going to be just for those who can afford it."

The words were no sooner out of his mouth than Titus fired back, "Trout fishing is not just for the rich. The working man has just as much right to fish for trout as corporate presidents!"

Hazzard jumped into the fray: "You can catch all the trout you want, Opie, if every fisherman carefully releases every fish he hooks."

"I wasn't thinking of creating an elitism on the river," Mason interjected. "I want the South Branch open to fly fishing. I'm told that flies-only regulations should help perpetuate the wild trout populations in streams like the South Branch and Au Sable for all anglers and for future generations."

There you have it: Perpetuating wild trout for future generations. That evening in his house on the eleven miles of the South Branch and on the 1,400 acres that he would (on his death four years later) bequeath to the state for public fishing access, Mason articulated the philosophy that would guide Griffith and the other founders of the organization that would become, nine years later, Trout Unlimited.

Mason died in October 1954, and Griffith took up the cause. On July

"Take care of the fish and the fishing will take care of itself."

18, 1959, in the Barbless Hook, his cottage on the Au Sable, Griffith and fourteen other anglers decided the time was ripe to found Trout Unlimited. Griffith was elected chairman. Vic Beresford, who had recently been fired as editor of *Michigan Out-of-Doors* for an editorial critical of state funding for conservation, was named secretary and would become TU's first executive director in a few short months. Others participating included Fred Bear, founder of Bear Archery; Casey E. Westell, Jr., who was to be elected TU's first president; Lon B. Adams, originator of the Adams pattern found in every dry fly box; and Art Neuman, founding vice president and maker of Wanigas Rods, hot items among those who love—and use today—antique tackle. Beresford spread the word and TU chapters blossomed in Illinois, New York, Pennsylvania, and Wisconsin.

A spate of activity followed the July meeting leading to the formal founding of Trout, Unlimited (the comma fell by the wayside in a few years) on September 5, 1959. Papers of incorporation were filed two weeks later. Not a month after its first meeting, TU passed a resolution calling on Michigan to complete a full inventory of its trout waters and their ability to sustain wild trout. A week later, on October 9, TU created a board of review of six prominent biologists to provide counsel on strategies for trout management and projects to be undertaken.

Founding members of the board were Karl T. Lagler, professor of fisheries management, School of Natural Resources, University of Michigan; Paul R. Needhal, professor of zoology-fisheries, Department of Zoology, University of California, Berkeley; and (previously mentioned) Albert S. Hazzard, assistant executive director, Pennsylvania Fish Commission. From its very beginning, TU has been committed to basing its conservation of native and wild trout and their habitats on good science. In December 1959, to a crowd of 250 gathered at TU's first general membership meeting, held at the High Life Inn in Saginaw, Griffith opened the meeting paraphrasing the opening stanza of Reinhold Niebuhr's Serenity Prayer: "God grant us the serenity to accept the things we cannot change, courage to change the things we can, and wisdom to know the difference."

Truth be told, TU has had a hard time with the serenity part of the prayer, but not courage or wisdom. TU was born because Mason and Griffith had seen the quality of angling decline on the Au Sable. Gone, to a large degree, were the wild browns of a pound or more that they'd known in the 1930s and '40s. What remained were stocked trout, anemic browns, and brookies that, according to Griffith, scarcely lasted a month. Not only was the mortality rate high, but the cost of producing hatchery fish consumed much of the Commission's budget. So much, in fact, that habitat improvement was all but ignored.

Griffith's first battle, soon after he and Mason had planted the seed for TU, was protecting the eight-mile run from Burton's Landing to Wakeley Bridge with fly fishing only, catch-and-release regulations. Most anglers were incensed. Their God-given right to take home a mess of trout was at stake. Griffith used his clout on the Commission to press for the conservation regs which were placed on the stretch in 1952. Subsequent studies of the Au Sable showed that the fish population had rebounded. Seven years later, he and the leadership of nascent TU pressed for and were able to extend the special regulations for five more years. TU was out of the chute.

TU won case before U.S. Supreme Court blocking construction of Tellico Dam on the Little Tennessee River and spearhead a campaign to end planning for the Allenspur Dam which would have flooded thirty-one miles of the Yellowstone's famed Paradise Valley.

• TU and U.S. Department of Interior held the first Wild Trout Symposium in Yellowstone National Park. Operation Restore, predecessor to Embrace-A-Stream and designed to foster chapter-based conservation projects, was funded by a $50,000 grant from the Richard King Mellon foundation. Embrace-A-Stream, by the end of 2007, would fund 800 projects and devote $8.4 million in cash and in-kind contributions to habitat restoration.

1979–1988

• Little Tennessee flooded after Senator Howard Baker attached rider to fund completion of Tellico Dam to bill signed by President Jimmy Carter. TU joined battle against construction of "Big A" dam at Ambejackmockmas Falls on the West Branch of the Penobscot, and Great Northern Paper dropped plans for the dam in 1985. Two Forks Dam, which would have flooded twenty miles of the South Platte including the famed Gold Medal section, was defeated by coalition led by TU.

• Wallop-Breaux Amendment to the Federal Aid to Sportfish Restoration Act supported by TU resulted in increased funding for state fishery programs. Pilot Colorado TU program expands into nationwide partnership with U.S. Forest Service to improve fisheries on lands it controls.

• Membership reached 50,000 and national office moved to Washington, D.C.

TU Milestones

1959–1968

• TU National Board of Review prepared a brief advocating managing streams for wild trout. As a result, Michigan increased the number of catch-and-release streams. Michigan began to cut back on stocking and increased funding for habitat improvement.

• West Slope Chapter of TU, led by George Grant, brought to a halt Bureau of Reclamation plans to construct Reichle Dam, saving twenty miles of Montana's Big Hole River from inundation. TU supported listing Apache and Gila trout and greenback and Pauite cutthroats as endangered species.

1969–1978

• National office moved from Michigan to Denver, Colorado. Canadian anglers established Trout Unlimited Canada.

• Bureau of Reclamation's planned Teton Dam near Newdale, Idaho, was vigorously protested by TU. But TU ran out of money, construction continued, and the dam failed on July 5, 1976, killing fourteen.

SALMON POOL, PENOBSCOT RIVER, BANGOR, MAINE

1989–1998

- Charles Gauvin became TU's Executive Director, TU founder Griffith died at ninety-seven, and membership passed 100,000.

- The U.N., under pressure from a number of conservation organizations including TU, banned indiscriminate netting of Pacific salmon.

- Bureau of Land Management, Forest Service, Fish and Wildlife Service, and TU created Bring Back the Natives to restore native fish, and TU sued California Department of Fish and Game forcing study of its trout stocking program. Big Blackfoot Chapter with Orvis and the National Fish and Wildlife Foundation launched $1 million campaign to restore the river made famous by Norman Maclean's *A River Runs Through It and Other Stories*.

- TU fielded its first Home Rivers Initiative—a broad conservation effort addressing conservation, and other economic and social goals—on the Beaverkill and Willowemoc watershed. Similar initiatives would be initiated on the Boise River, Snake River (Colorado) Potomac headwaters, Bear River, American Fork, South Fork Snake River, Jefferson River, Kettle Creek, and West Fork Kickapoo River.

- Northeast Kingdom Chapter achieved victory when it (and allies in Vermont) obtained ruling from the Federal Energy Regulatory Commission (FERC) that Newport No. 11 Dam on the Clyde River would not be relicensed. Also in New England, the Kennebec River Chapter and a coalition of champions for Maine natural resources secured

FERC's agreement that the Edwards Dam at Augusta should be removed. The structure was taken out in 1999, opening seventeen miles of river to salmon, shad, striped bass, and alewives.

- Western Water Project wass initiated with the opening of offices in Boulder, Colorado, and Missoula, Montana. Offices have been added in Idaho, Utah, and Wyoming. Professional staff, TU volunteers, and public and private sector partners since have brokered agreements that stabilize sustainable stream flows, remove or mitigate barriers to migrating trout and salmon, and build political will to forestall large-scale mining, oil and gas drilling, and timbering ventures that threaten water quality.

- "Hands Across the Border," a joint report from Trout Unlimited and Trout Unlimited Canada, offered recommendations to resolve the stalemate on implementation of the Pacific Salmon Treaty.

- A week-long conservation and fishing camp for youth on Pennsylvania's Yellow Breeches Creek, founded by the Cumberland Valley Chapter in 1995, immersed high-school-aged students in stream ecology, fisheries science, and techniques for successful fly and spin fishing. Today, more than a dozen state councils operate summer coldwater conservation camps.

Growing youth into angler-conservationists will sustain the future of Trout Unlimited. (upper right)

For twenty years, Trout Unlimited has flourished under the leadership of Charles Gauvin, its staff of talented professionals, and thousands of dedicated volunteers. (lower left)

1999–2008

- Back the Brookie, conceived as a campaign to engage citizens of North Carolina and Tennessee to restore the southern Appalachian brook trout and fight for stronger clean air and water laws, evolved into TU's largest conservation initiative: the Eastern Brook Trout Joint Venture. The venture united seventeen states, six federal agencies, a number of universities, and hundreds of TU chapters and thousands of members in the restoration of the brook trout to its home waters from Maine to Georgia. TU's campaign, Strategies for Restoring Native Trout, succeed in re-establishing Bonneville and Lahontan cutthroats in streams in Idaho, Nevada, and Wyoming.

- With funding from the Tiffany Foundation, TU, Snowbird Resorts, and the Forest Service cleaned up Pacific Mine in American Fork Canyon, creating a model for mitigation of drainage and tailings from more than 500,000 abandoned hard-rock mines in the West. As this is being written, TU and a host of collaborators are fighting the creation of an Alaskan gold mining district as big as the state of Rhode Island that threatens to eliminate Pacific salmon from the headwaters of Bristol Bay. Unless TU and its partners are successful, 12,500 jobs that provide the sole livelihood for residents of small towns and villages in Southwest Alaska will be lost.

- In addition, the West Branch Susquehanna Restoration Initiative has built on the 1998 Kettle Creek Home Rivers Initiative and is developing plans and securing funding to address acid seepage from old coal mines in a 7,000-square-mile area of Pennsylvania's Appalachian Highlands.

- Ever seeking a balance between the needs of society overall and the imperative to conserve valuable natural resources, TU members and staff encouraged Congress to pass legislation permanently protecting the Rocky Mountain Front from oil and gas drilling. President George W. Bush has signed legislation prohibiting oil and gas development in 40,000 acres of New Mexico's Carson National Forest, known as the Valley Vidal. Both measures protect populations of native cutthroat trout.

- Increasingly, TU chapters and councils are developing curricula that interface with state standards of learning so that educators can include lessons about conserving mountain streams and spring creeks as they teach. Trout in the Classroom, the program where school children learn about the development of fish from egg to fingerling and then stock the trout they've raised, can be found in more than 300 schools nationwide.

- To measure quantitatively whether its conservation initiatives are achieving their goals, TU is developing the Conservation Success Index (CSI). The CSI melds population data from trout assessments completed by state and federal agencies with spatial data on habitat and threats gathered by TU's staff scientists to create a common analytical framework applicable to all native coldwater salmonids. This approach allows TU to direct organizational resources to the places that are most in need and where the greatest conservation benefits can be achieved. The CSI is being integrated with GIS programs used by most governmental agencies and conservation organizations to enhance planning at local, regional, state, and national levels.

The Future

- As it enters its second half-century, Trout Unlimited knows that the environment faces massive challenges from global warming, competition for water, and the quest for supplies of energy. To meet these challenges, TU is committed to developing strategies based on the best science and with a broad understanding of social and economic impacts.

To guide it into the future, TU has defined goals in four broad themes: *Protect* watersheds to ensure the highest quality habitat for native and wild fish; *Reconnect* fragmented streams to sustain healthy populations of native and wild fish; *Restore* degraded coldwater habitat through collaboration with landowners and other stakeholders; and *Sustain* conservation efforts by building capacity within all levels of TU with a particular emphasis on enabling young people to successfully engage in long-term conservation efforts so that TU's legacy will endure beyond the current generation.

Volunteers from Dominion, an energy company; the Roanoke Valley Chapter of Trout Unlimited; and staff from the U. S. Forest Service and the Virginia Department of Game and Inland Fisheries demonstrate the public-private partnerships on which conservation success depends.

Acknowledgments

The person to whom I'm most grateful is my wife, Katie Anders. I'm sure she regrets her suggestion twelve years ago that I take a year off and write. Instead I fished and became infected with Trout Unlimited. But she's ever gracious, always of good cheer, and can spot a comma-splice at a thousand paces. I'm more fortunate than I possibly deserve.

Charles Gauvin, Whit Fosburgh, Steve Moyer, and Chris Wood of Trout Unlimited all were instrumental in conceiving this project as a principal component of TU's 50th anniversary. When the project stumbled and current poured into its waders, Beth Duris, editor of *Trout*, and Jim Gray, the magazine's extremely talented art director, grabbed its suspenders and got it back on its feet. Without their help, we would simply have no book.

Jay Cassell, an old friend and editor of *Trout Unlimited's Guide to America's 100 Best Trout Streams*, connected me with Tony Lyons, president of Skyhorse Publishing, and *Rivers of Restoration* was launched. Jay edited the text and saved me as he always does from my sins. Invaluable assistance has been provided by Tony, Abigail Gehring, Adam Bozarth, and their team at Skyhorse.

Others who personally helped with this project are legion. I can't hope to name them all. You'll find many of their names in the book. Among those unstinting in their aid were Luki Akelkok, Walter Babb, Stan Bradshaw, Tim Bristol, Matt Bond, Chuck Bonham, Steve Born, Pat Coffin, Joe Congleton, Rob Dickerson, Don Duff, Bruce Farling, Ted Fitzgerald, Nat Gillespie, Annette Hartigan, Jeff Hastings, Roy Hawk, Michael Heck, Carl Heuter, Laura Hewitt, Mike Holt, Dan Kenny, Mike Klimkos, Brian Kraft, Dennis Labare, Sharon and Mark Lance, Shaun Lawson, Bob Linsenman, Kirt Mayland, Mick McCorcle, Harold McMillan, Steve Melton, Alan Moore, Steve Moore, Rick Murphree, Kristin Pelz, John Pickard, Michael Piquette, Zyg Plater, Chris Radke, Don Ratliff, Rob Roberts, Russ Schnitzer, Squeak Smith, Scott Vance, Amy Wolfe, Ted Wood, Matt Woodard, Marcia Woolman, and Laura Zeimer.

In the end, though, it's TU's 150,000 members, the staff of every federal and state agency that stewards trout and salmon waters, elected officials who support sound environmental policies, and corporations and foundations that fund conservation work who deserve credit for this book. They are the ones who get the job done.

INDEX

Photos by John Ross appear on pages 3, 5, 6, 7, 11, 12, 13, 14, 18, 21, 24, 32, 37, 41, 43, 45, 46, 57, 58, 65, 66, 67, 71, 72, 96, 98, 101, 103, 105, 111, 112, 119, and 125